Graham Greene, Ireland and the Honorary Consul

STUDIES IN FRANCO-IRISH RELATIONS

VOLUME 23

SERIES EDITOR

Dr Eamon Maher,
Technological University Dublin – Tallaght Campus

Graham Greene, Ireland and the Honorary Consul

A View from the South of France

Pierre Joannon

PETER LANG
Oxford · Berlin · Bruxelles · Chennai · Lausanne · New York

Bibliographic information published by the Deutsche Nationalbibliothek.
The German National Library lists this publication in the German National
Bibliography; detailed bibliographic data is available on the Internet
at http://dnb.d-nb.de.

A catalogue record for this book is available from the British Library.

Library of Congress Cataloging-in-Publication Data

Names: Joannon, Pierre, author.
Title: Graham Greene, Ireland and the honorary consul : a view from the south of France / Pierre Joannon.
Description: Oxford ; NewYork : Peter Lang, 2024. | Series: Studies in Franco-Irish relations, 1864273X ; 23 | Includes bibliographical references.
Identifiers: LCCN 2023054666 (print) | LCCN 2023054667 (ebook) | ISBN 9781803744230 (paperback) | ISBN 9781803744247 (ebook) | ISBN 9781803744254 (epub)
Subjects: LCSH: Greene, Graham, 1904-1991. | Novelists, English—20th century—Biography. | Ireland—Intellectual life. | LCGFT: Biographies.
Classification: LCC PR6013.R44 Z63446 2024 (print) | LCC PR6013.R44 (ebook) | DDC 823/.912 [B]—dc23/eng/20231129
LC record available at https://lccn.loc.gov/2023054666
LC ebook record available at https://lccn.loc.gov/2023054667

Cover image: Photograph of Graham Greene taken by Louis Monier.
Louis MONIER/GAMMA RAPHO.
Cover design by Peter Lang Group AG

ISSN 1864-273X
ISBN 978-1-80374-423-0 (print)
ISBN 978-1-80374-424-7 (ePDF)
ISBN 978-1-80374-425-4 (ePub)
DOI 10.3726/b21264

© 2024 Peter Lang Group AG, Lausanne
Published by Peter Lang Ltd, Oxford, United Kingdom
info@peterlang.com - www.peterlang.com

Pierre Joannon has asserted his right under the Copyright, Designs and Patents Act, 1988, to be identified as Author of this Work.

All rights reserved.
All parts of this publication are protected by copyright.
Any utilisation outside the strict limits of the copyright law, without the permission of the publisher, is forbidden and liable to prosecution.
This applies in particular to reproductions, translations, microfilming, and storage and processing in electronic retrieval systems.

This publication has been peer reviewed.

' – I like "The Honorary Consul" best.
– You didn't write that after you'd met our Honorary Consul, Pierre Joannon?
– No! At least I don't think so, although I have known him a long time, he's quite unique. And I was a founder of the Jameson Irish Club here with him.'

Elgy Gillespie, 'Graham Greene at home',
The Irish Times, 25 July 1981

Photograph of Graham Greene signed to Pierre and Annick Joannon.

Contents

List of Illustrations	ix
Preface by Eamon Maher	xi
Acknowledgements	xxi
An Encounter in Antibes	1
Ways of Escape	9
A Stroll in Ireland after the Civil War	15
An Idyll in Achill	21
A Most Peculiar Relationship	29
A Foray in Northern Ireland	35
Irish Poets, Novelists and Peacemakers	45
Antibes, the Town Greene Loved So Well	49
Meeting the Irish	53
The Final Challenge	65
A Literary Feud	73
Last Encounter	81
Interviews and Obituaries: Graham Greene's Other Island	87

The Sage of Antibes	99
Our Man in Antibes	103
Bibliography	105

Illustrations

Photograph of Graham Greene signed to Pierre and Annick Joannon.	vi
Graham Greene taking his breakfast on the terrace of his flat on the fourth floor of the Résidence des Fleurs overlooking the harbour of Antibes and the Fort Carré.	5
Graham Greene and Suzanne Joannon, Les Chênes Verts, Cap d'Antibes, 27 September 1980.	8
Launch of the Jameson Irish Club at the Hotel Helios in Juan les Pins, 26 September 1980. From left to right: Irish painter Louis Le Brocquy; Jacqueline Murphy; Graham Greene; Irish Film Censor Sheamus Smith; future Taoiseach Garret FitzGerald; Pierre Joannon; French writer Paul Guimard; Annick Joannon; French writer Michel Déon of the Académie française; French writer Benoite Groult.	54
John Ryan offering a bottle of Jameson Irish Whiskey to Graham Greene in the presence of Yvonne Cloetta (Juan les Pins, 26 September 1980).	55
Michel Déon of the Académie française, Pierre Joannon and Graham Greene, September 1980.	56
Lady Glenavy; Irish Film Censor Sheamus Smith; Lord Glenavy known as Paddy Campbell; Sheila Hampson; Annick Joannon; Graham Greene (Villa Dinah, Juan les Pins, 25 April 1980).	58
Graham Greene; Pierre Joannon; Lady Glenavy (Villa Dinah, Parc Saramarte, Juan les Pins, 25 April 1980).	60
John Boorman; Pierre Joannon and Graham Greene at the Villa Les Chênes Verts in the Cap d'Antibes, for the launching of John Boorman's film *Excalibur* at the International Cannes Film festival, 24 May 1981.	63

Graham Greene, Pierre Joannon and Anthony Burgess at Eden Roc, Cap d'Antibes, 18 May 1982.	64
Letter of Graham Greene to General Raoul Salan, 8 April 1980.	68
Pierre Joannon, Graham Greene, Martine and Yvonne Cloetta at Les Chênes Verts, Cap d'Antibes, 24 May 1981.	71
Graham Greene, John Banville, Tony Ryan and Desmond O'Malley, GPA Book Award, 28 November 1989.	76
Graham Greene speaking at the GPA Book Award, Dublin 28 November 1989.	77
Plaque on the façade of the Résidence des Fleurs, 26 Avenue Pasteur, Antibes.	84

Preface by Eamon Maher

There are times when being General Editor of a book series provides opportunities to publish work in areas that are close to one's heart. This is certainly the case with Pierre Joannon's insightful description of the special friendship between himself and the renowned English Catholic writer Graham Greene (1904–1991), which I saw immediately as being a great fit for *Studies in Franco-Irish Relations* series, mainly because Pierre Joannon has been such a powerhouse and promoter of Irish Studies in France over several decades, but also because of my life-long interest in Graham Greene.

However, before extolling some of the obvious merits of this publication, I think it is important to share with you the multiple achievements of its author, who is really someone whose contribution to strengthening Franco-Irish links is of inestimable value to the smaller of these two Celtic cousins. It is only fitting that this work resulted in Pierre being given Irish citizenship in 1997 and receiving France's highest award, the *Légion d'Honneur*, in 2002. His *Histoire de l'Irlande et des Irlandais* (2006) is considered compulsory reading for any French person seeking to understand Irish history and its people. He has also published the only biographies in French of Michael Collins and John Hume, as well as a host of other books, most notably in terms of the present study, two key publications dealing with the close ties with Ireland of famous French figures Charles de Gaulle[1] and Michel Déon.[2] He also wrote a brilliant evocation of the capital city of Ireland entitled *Il était une fois Dublin*[3] and was co-editor, with Kevin Whelan, of *Paris, Capital of Irish Culture*, the proceedings of

---

1   Pierre Joannon, *L'Hiver du Connétable: Charles de Gaulle et l'Irlande* (Orléans : Regain de Lecture/Corsaire Éditions, 2023).
2   Pierre Joannon, *Une amitié vagabonde* (La Thébaïde: Raincy, 2019).
3   Pierre Joannon, *Il était une fois Dublin* (Paris: Perrin, 2013). *The Irish Times*, although it has a policy of not reviewing books in languages other than English and Irish, ran a review by me on this title.

two conferences held in Dublin and Paris, which were published by Four Courts Press in November 2017.[4] This is just a sample of the work that Pierre has done; indeed, the whole Preface could be given over to describing all of them and their significance.

An indication of the esteem in which Pierre is held can be seen in his election to the Royal Irish Academy in March 2021, a richly deserved accolade for someone who has dedicated much of his adult life to promoting Irish Studies in France and farther afield. So, readers of this book will appreciate what a genuine honour it is for me to write a Preface to the fascinating reminiscences of the Honorary Consul General of Ireland in the South–East of France since 1973 and the author of *The Honorary Consul*, Greene's highly regarded work of fiction, which, coincidentally, was also published in 1973.

Destiny would decree that the paths of these two men would cross, as they both had an apartment in the Résidence des Fleurs, overlooking the resplendent harbour of Antibes on the much-vaunted Côte d'Azur in France. Pierre's intimate knowledge of Irish history and politics (he was completing a PhD on the subject at the time they first met), as well as the amazing network of Irish writers, politicians, artists and people from the business world that he was building up, made it inevitable in some way that Greene would, in his turn, meet and befriend a number of these people. Another factor in bringing the two men closer was the fact that in 1971 Greene had written a letter to *The Times* that was critical of the sensory deprivation techniques that were being employed in Northern Ireland by the British army and the RUC at that awful time during the Troubles. The letter was seen by Pierre, who approved of the brave position that Greene adopted as a former member of the British Secret Service. Serendipity works in strange ways and on occasions causes the paths of people to coalesce in a manner they might never have imagined possible.

What most appeals to me in Pierre's moving personal account of a growing friendship, which is what the French would call '*un témoignage*', is the degree to which it reveals Greene's deep relationship with Ireland,

---

4 Pierre Joannon and Kevin Whelan (eds), *Paris, Capital of Irish Culture* (Dublin: Four Courts Press, 2017).

something which, to my knowledge, has not been done to date. There are certainly brief references to Ireland in Norman Sherry's magisterial three-tome biography of Greene,[5] but nothing that could compare to the detailed accounts that Pierre provides and that are the fruit of his having first-hand knowledge of what turns out to be Greene's significant association with the Emerald Isle. Ernie O'Malley, Seán O'Faoláin, Conor Cruise O'Brien, Gerry Fitt, John Hume, Garret FitzGerald, Patrick Campbell and a host of other dignitaries are all mentioned as people whom Greene encountered, some described in more detail than others according to their significance, but all utterly absorbing. Achill Island features as the location where Greene spent a whole month with his mistress Catherine Walston in 1947, but his stay in Mayo also led to his becoming close friends with Ernie O'Malley at this time. It seems to me that Tourism Ireland is missing a trick in not using Greene's close association with Achill as a means of bringing more visitors to that idyllic part of Ireland in a similar way to how Heinrich Böll's sojourn and *The Banshees of Inisherin* are employed in publicity campaigns for the island.

In addition, one will read about encounters between Greene and Michel Déon, a member of the Académie Française and a renowned French writer who lived for a long period in Tynagh, Co. Galway, and about the admiration he expressed for the Belfast writer Brian Moore (1921–1999), whom he famously described on more than one occasion as his 'favourite living author', an amazing compliment to someone who, in spite of his obvious literary talents, was never close to matching up to a novelist of Greene's stature. In some regards, however, one can see why there would be an affinity between the two writers, as both delved into the dilemmas faced by their characters when they begin to doubt their Catholic faith. They also probed the difficult relationships between men and women, political intrigue in various countries around the world and the strains caused by colonial oppression: in many ways, they were global writers *d'avant la lettre*. Vincent McDonnell and John Banville are equally given

---

5   Norman Sherry, *The Life of Graham Greene* (London: Pimlico/Jonathan Cape, 2004).

honourable mention as the writers who in 1988 were somewhat controversially named joint recipients of the GPA (Guinness Peat Aviation) Book Award, for which Greene acted as Chair of the judging panel. The prize, worth a whopping £50,000, was the brainchild of Dr Tony Ryan, who went on to enjoy a lucrative career in aviation culminating in the setting up of the highly successful low-cost airline, Ryanair, and was a generous patron of the arts in Ireland.

The book is replete with gorgeous vignettes of soirées organised by Pierre or Graham (more often the former) where literati rubbed shoulders with successful people from the world of business and politics, and the best hospitality was available in abundance to guests – the photos supplied by Pierre show elegantly dressed people enjoying plentiful supplies of food and drink and clearly enjoying themselves immensely. In many cases, it is like a Who's Who on the Côte d'Azur, without the distasteful presence of photographers from *Paris-Match* or *Hello* magazines.

When I was in secondary school, my father, who was an English teacher and staunch Catholic, recommended that I read some of Greene's novels. Strangely enough, given the racy content (for the Ireland of the 1970s, that is!) of books like *Brighton Rock* or *The End of the Affair*, for some reason best known to himself, my father considered Greene a 'safe' writer. I feel it had something to do with the fact that Greene was a Catholic, albeit an English version of that religious grouping, and someone who wrote beautiful prose – my father was always attracted to writers with a clear, concise style. Whatever his reasons were, this paternal recommendation sparked a life-long engagement with the 'Catholic Novel', a description that is often rejected by those most closely associated with it, including Greene himself, the American Flannery O'Connor, the French Nobel Laureate François Mauriac and the French-American writer Julien Green, all of whom declared that they were not Catholic writers so such, more writers who also happened to be Catholic.

One of the key works in this area is undoubted that of Conor Cruise O'Brien, who published under the nom de plume Donat O'Donnell the highly regarded study, *Maria Cross: Imaginative Patterns in a Group of Modern Catholic Writers*, which features French authors in the main, but also the English writers Evelyn Waugh and Graham Greene, and, somewhat

Preface by Eamon Maher

surprisingly in my mind, Seán O'Faoláin on the Irish side – I think Liam O'Flaherty or Kate O'Brien would have been far more obvious choices. O'Donnell's main focus, as revealed by the title of his book (Maria Cross is the name of the heroine in Mauriac's novel, *Le Désert de l'amour*), was on the French exponents of Catholic literature, and especially Mauriac. The treatment of Greene concentrates largely on the theme of pity in *The Heart of the Matter*, a novel set in an English colonial outpost on the West coast of Africa. The main protagonist, a police officer called Scobie, is torn between his devotion to his wife, Louise, who hates life in what she considers an intolerable backwater and wants to escape to South Africa, and a young woman called Helen Rolt. Scobie borrows money from a Syrian, Yusef, a suspected criminal who has been on the police radar for some time, to cover the boat fare to South Africa for Louise. But Scobie's difficulties are compounded when he becomes involved, out of pity more than lust, in an adulterous relationship with Mrs Rolt, who ends up living 500 yards from his house. He is then forced, when his wife returns unexpectedly from South Africa, to receive Holy Communion while in a state of mortal sin in order to convince Louise that the rumours of his infidelity are unfounded. As a practicing Catholic, Scobie knows the consequences of his act (he repeats the sacrilege on a few more occasions), but his fate is sealed when he decides to commit suicide, the ultimate sin for a Catholic.

Scobie wonders why an all-loving God should demand that he inflict pain on his innocent female victims: '… how can one love God at the expense of one of his creatures? Would a woman accept the love for which a child had to be sacrificed?'[6] At the end of the novel, speaking with Louise about her deceased husband, Father Rank refuses to pronounce on Scobie's fate: 'For goodness sake, Mrs Scobie', he says, 'don't imagine you – or I – know a thing about God's mercy.'[7] In an analysis that would seem to borrow heavily on Greene's own view that the rules of the Church often neglect to engage with what goes on in the human heart, the priest intimates that God might not judge Scobie's suicide as harshly as one

---

6   Graham Greene, *The Heart of the Matter* (London: Penguin Books, 1966; original edition Heinemann, 1948), 179.
7   Greene, *Heart of the Matter*, 263.

might think: 'It may seem an odd thing to say – when a man's as wrong as he (Scobie) was – but I think from what I saw of him, that he really loved God.' To which Louise retorts: 'He certainly loved no one else.'[8] This is not altogether true: on countless occasions Scobie is portrayed as being more attracted to the brokenness and vulnerability of his wife and mistress than he is to anything sexual. He feels called on to bring healing to those in pain and in the end he can see no alternative to taking his own life in an attempt to free the two women from his continued toxic presence and to end what he considers a useless existence. His dialogues with Jesus on the Cross indicate that he sees himself as inflicting even more pain on God through his actions, but the reality is that his motivation is to try and help others to avoid suffering, not to inflict it.

O'Donnell maintains that *The Heart of the Matter* satisfies Jacques Maritain's fundamental requirement for the Catholic novel – compassionate understanding of the sinner without collusion with the sin[9] – but one wonders if such an approach is satisfactory to the Irish academic and critic. The way in which Greene suggests that for all his human failings and his decision to take his own life, Scobie may well be a saint, is a theology of grace that was not very widespread in Ireland or indeed in France during the 1950s and 1960s, which may explain how Greene never made as great an impression in my home country as someone like Mauriac, whose Jansenist distrust of sins of the flesh was much closer to the Irish tradition. In addition, Greene's conversion to Catholicism did not mean that he completely abandoned his Anglican upbringing and one encounters in many instances a more positive interpretation of Catholic dogma in his work than one finds in Irish writers at the time. O'Donnell makes the following point about Mauriac: 'He had not been free to choose or reject Catholicism for he was born a Catholic …; the faith had reached him principally through a mother who was a formidable emotional force; he, too, had been torn between "the inclinations of an ardent nature", and

---

8   Greene, *Heart of the Matter*, 264.
9   Donat O'Donnell, *Maria Cross: Imaginative Patterns in a Group of Modern Catholic Writers* (London: Chatto & Windus, 1954), 84.

Preface by Eamon Maher

grace.'[10] This observation shows the similarity between Mauriac and the vast majority of Irish writers who happened to be practicing Catholics. Conscious of his unhealthy preoccupation with concupiscence, Mauriac determined to prevent his work from becoming a vehicle for opening a path to sin for his readers.

Greene and Mauriac were inevitably aware of each other's work and regularly commented on aspects that they admired in various publications as they appeared in English and French translation. An example of this is Mauriac's extremely positive Preface to the French translation of *The Power and the Glory*, in which he makes a number of revealing comments. The first is that, as distinct from an English Catholic like Greene, the French Catholic has to come to terms with a long history of polemics that marked the Catholic Church in his country: the struggle between Port-Royal and the Jesuits, whether one supported Bossuet or Fénelon, or espoused the theology of Lamennais and Lacordaire over that of Louis Veuillot. According to Mauriac, Greene entered into the mysterious world of grace and human nature without any of the baggage that would mark a French Catholic. He could therefore produce a model in the whisky priest (the hero or anti-hero of *The Power and the Glory*) of a very imperfect man who is nonetheless a conduit for grace. 'He knows he is a man so ordinary, so mediocre in every way that his sins only cause people to shrug their shoulders when they speak of him. And yet what this extraordinary book shows us is the use of sin by divine Grace.'[11]

Mauriac was often criticised, and with some justification, for presenting sin and the sinner in a positive manner, for even conniving with the Devil at times. At a certain point in his career, and following the advice of Jacques Maritain, he decided to 'purify the source', that is to say, he would continue giving life to characters who were often eaten up with evil, but he would do so with a pure heart. However, his particular form of art found more dramatic possibilities in portraying sinners than in attempting to depict

---

10   *Maria Cross*, 24–25.
11   Préface, *La Puissance et la Gloire* (Paris: Éditions Robert Laffont, 1948), 5–6. (My translation).

saints – Bernanos was more at home with the latter than any other novelist of the time, including Greene.

On one occasion, his friend André Gide remarked to Mauriac: 'The object of your novels is not so much to bring sinners to Christianity as to remind Christians that there is something on earth besides Heaven … Doubtless if I were more of a Christian I should be less your disciple.'[12] That thin line between religious conviction and artistic production was always something that caused Mauriac much angst and it was something he never fully resolved. Irish novelists of the 1940s, 1950s and 1960s were in the main at variance with a Catholic Church that tried to exert control over what they could justifiably write about in their books. There was much concern about broaching subjects that could pose a danger to public morality, sex being to the forefront in this regard. Writing about O'Faoláin, O'Donnell notes:

> It is exceedingly difficult to be a Catholic writer in a Catholic country: the pressure of a community varies inversely with its size; ingrowing nationalism destroys a writer's scope. Mr. O'Faoláin has been a living example of the truth and interrelation of these three propositions. He does not have to refute them all together in order to rediscover his direction as a writer. He may have to fly to the ends of the earth.[13]

Many Irish writers were forced to emigrate with a view to escaping the repressive influence of Church and State. Several, most notably Joyce and Beckett, ended up in Paris, a city where writers and artists were revered in a way that was not the case in Ireland. It seems to me that Graham Greene acts as a sort of buffer between the fierce, unthinking attachment to Catholicism that once characterised the southern state of Ireland, and the more philosophical, rational, even theological approach of the French, who from an early age were encouraged to question and to seek out answers to the problems that life threw at them, especially in the religious domain. This Preface has paid a lot of attention to the portrayal of Catholicism in the novel because in some ways it shows the reason why a writer like Mauriac was much more likely to appeal to the Irish

12 Cited by O'Donnell, *Maria Cross*, 6.
13 *Maria Cross*, 114–115.

sensibility than someone like Greene. That said, thanks to this wonderfully insightful book by Pierre Joannon, we can now see that our neighbour from across the Irish Sea understood the Irish mentality very well and was in many ways attracted to our customs and practices. How else could he have had such a close relationship with someone as steeped in Irish history and culture as Pierre Joannon, who is at one and the same time French and Irish?

By making France his main abode for the latter years of his life, Graham Greene may well have had a similar objective to those Irish writers who fled their country of birth in search of a more tolerant mode of existence. But there is no doubt in my mind that his affinity with Ireland owes much to his friend Pierre Joannon, who acted as Greene's confidant and gentle guide, a type of surrogate Honorary Consul revealing some of the hidden mysteries of the Emerald Isle. The two men had much in common: they were intelligent, witty, alert to what was happening in the world. They liked the occasional glass of good wine, whiskey or beer, exchanging anecdotes over a nice meal, and were very comfortable in gatherings of polite society. They were also Catholics, one by birth, the other by choice, which inevitably created a certain understanding of the other's world view. From the celestial perch on which he now rests, I am sure that Graham is more than happy with Pierre's account of their friendship and I sense his spirit inhabits the pages that you are about to read. For my part, I am confident that you will be as entranced as I was by the story Pierre recounts in a way that Greene himself would have been proud of.

Bonne lecture.
Eamon Maher, Director of the National Centre for Franco-Irish Studies, TU Dublin.

Acknowledgements

I especially want to thank Dr Eamon Maher, a dedicated and brilliant academic who has been ploughing the furrow of Franco-Irish relations for decades, for his guidance, for his Preface on a subject he knows particularly well, and for taking a gamble that some people might want to read a book on Graham Greene and Ireland.

I wish to express my gratitude to Francis Greene and David Higham Associates for their authorization to reproduce Graham Greene's letter to the editor of *The Times* dated 26th November 1971 and 'Impressions of Dublin', first published in the *Weekly Westminster Gazette* dated 25 August 1923.

I also thank Mike Hill, Director of the Graham Greene International Festival, and the Graham Greene Birthplace Trust, for having invited me to the 19th Graham Greene International Festival which took place between the 21st and the 24th of September 2017 in Berkhamsted School, Hertfordshire, UK, and for having encouraged me to expand my lecture at Greene's old school.

I am grateful to Judith Adamson, editor of Graham Greene *Reflections* (Reinhardt Books, London, 1990) for her observations and information on the GPA Book Award, and for attracting my attention to her fine essay in *Max Reinhardt. A Life in Publishing* (Palgrave Macmillan, Houndmills, Basingstoke, Hampshire, 2009).

I am also deeply indebted to Sean Donlon for his support and friendship and for his authorization to reproduce his letter to Graham Greene dated 9 March 1989, formalizing the discussions held at my house on the proposed GPA Book Award.

I am most grateful to Bernard Zeller and the Association des Amis de Raoul Salan for having granted me the authorization to reproduce Graham Greene's letters to General Salan dated 23 November 1951; 24 March 1980; and 8 April 1980.

I thank Cormac O'Malley for his assessment of the relationship between his father Ernie O'Malley, Graham Greene, and Catherine Walston and her husband.

I also wish to thank my friend Kevin Whelan for his practical advice and his editorial eye.

I would like finally to pay tribute to Professor Richard Greene of the University of Toronto (no relation to Graham), editor of *Graham Greene. A Life in Letters* (Little Brown Book Group, London 2007), and author of a recent, vivid, well researched and evenly balanced biography of the author of *The End of the Affair*. Entitled *Russian Roulette: The Life and Times of Graham Greene* (Little Brown, London, 2020), this biography at last does justice to its subject. Ian Thomson, author of *Articles of Faith. The collected Tablet journalism of Graham Greene* (Signal Books, Oxford, 2006) wrote in *The Evening Standard* of 3 September 2020 a perceptive review to which there is nothing to add in my opinion:

> Thank goodness for Richard Greene, whose splendid one-volume biography offers a succinct counterbalance to Sherry's inedible trifle and conjures the man Evelyn Waugh nicknamed 'Grisjambon Vert' (French for 'grey ham green') in all his perplexing variety. Where Sherry is tactless and indecorous, Richard Greene is respectful and considered. Crisply written, *Russian Roulette* takes its title from Greene's vaunted flirtation with suicide as a teenager in Berkhamsted outside London, where his father was a school headmaster … Cogently argued and happily free of jargon, *Russian Roulette* offers a long-needed antidote to 'dirty linen' biographers who have sought to expose a darker shade of Greene and, in consequence, lost sight of the books. At last Graham Greene has the biographer he deserves.

An Encounter in Antibes

I first met Graham Greene some years before I was appointed Irish Honorary Consul in 1973, the same year in which Greene published what he considered to be his finest novel, *The Honorary Consul*. In the early nineteen seventies, we were both living in the Résidence des Fleurs, an apartment block overlooking Antibes harbour in the south of France. I was completing my doctorate on the constitutions and politics of the republic of Ireland. Unable to purchase Irish newspapers in Antibes, I was forced to rely on the London *Times* to follow Irish events North and South.

On 26 November 1971, I was amazed to read a letter to *The Times* written by a neighbour in the Résidence des Fleurs, one Graham Greene whom I knew by sight but had never spoken to. Greene denounced the sensory deprivation techniques, known euphemistically as 'clean torture', deployed on fourteen internees by the British army and the Royal Ulster Constabulary at Ballykelly army base in Co. Derry in Northern Ireland.[1] The letter is so indicative of Graham's character that I quote it in full:

> To be at the same time a Catholic and an Englishman is today to be ashamed on both counts. As a Catholic one is ashamed that more than a thousand years of Christianity has not abated the brutality of those Catholic women who shaved a young girl's head and poured tar and red lead over her body because she intended to marry an English soldier. As an Englishman the shame is even greater.
>
> 'Deep interrogation' – a bureaucratic phrase which takes the place of the simpler world 'torture' and is worthy of Orwell's *1984* – is on a different level of immorality from hysterical sadism of the indiscriminating bomb of the urban guerrillas. It is something organised with imagination and a knowledge of psychology, calculated and cold blooded, and it is only half condemned by the Compton investigation.

1 *The Times*, 26 November 1971; *New York Times*, 2 December 1971; Graham Greene, *Yours etc. Letters to the Press 1945–89*, selected and introduced by Christopher Hawtree (London: Reinhardt Books, 1989), 154–7.

Mr Maudling in his blithe jolly style, reminiscent of that used by defenders of corporal punishment when they remember their school days, suggests that no one has suffered permanent injury from this form of torture, by standing long hours pressed against a wall, hooded in darkness, isolated and deprived of hearing as well as sight by permanent noise, prevented in the intervals of the ordeal from sleep. These were the methods we condemned in the Slanski trials in Czechoslovakia and in the case of Cardinal Midzenty in Hungary.

Slanski is dead, he cannot be asked by Mr Maudling how permanent was the injury he suffered, but one would like to know the opinion of the Cardinal on methods which when applied by communists or fascists we call 'torture' and when applied by the British become downgraded to 'ill treatment'. If I, as a Catholic, were living in Ulster today I confess I would have one savage and irrational ambition – to see Mr Maudling pressed against a wall for hours on end, with a hood over his head, hearing nothing but the noise of a wind machine, deprived of sleep, and when the noise temporarily ceases by the bland voice of a politician telling him that his brain will suffer no irreparable damage.

The effects of these methods extend far beyond the borders of Ulster. How can any Englishman now protest against torture in Vietnam, in Greece, in Brazil, in the psychiatric wards of the USSR, without being told 'You have a double standard: one for others and another for your own country'.

And after all the British tortures and the Catholic outrages, what comes next? We all know the end of the story, however long the politicians keep up their parrot cry of 'no talk until violence ends'. When I was young it was the same cliché they repeated. Collins was 'a gunman and a thug'. 'We will not talk to murderers'. No one doubts that it was in our power then to hold Ireland by force. The Black and Tans matched the Republicans in terror. It was the English people who in the end forced the politicians to sit down at a table with 'the gunman and the thug'.

Now too, when the deaths and the tortures have gone on long enough to blacken us in the eyes of the world and to sicken even a Conservative of the right, there will inevitably be a temporary truce and a round-table conference – Mr Maudling or his successor will sit down over the coffee and the sandwiches with representatives of Éire and Stormont, of the IRA and the Provisional IRA to discuss with no pre-ordained conditions changes in the constitution and in the borders of Ulster. Why not now rather than later?

As a young lawyer with a particular interest in the fundamental principles of civil liberties, human rights as well as public and private freedoms in general, I followed closely the case of the so-called 'Hooded Men' which had provoked the angry reaction of my neighbour in the

Résidence des Fleurs. In 1976, the European Commission for Human rights declared that the use of the five sensory deprivation techniques denounced by Greene (hooding, stress positions, white noise, sleep deprivation and being deprived of food and water) amounted to torture. In 1978, the European Court of Human Rights reversed that decision, stating that the use of the five techniques used in combination for a long period fall into the category of inhuman treatment, but not torture. Prompted by revelations that British authorities withheld crucial information from the court in the original hearing and that the British government already knew at the time about the long-term psychological scarring of these five deprivation techniques, the Irish government decided in December 2014 to ask the Strasbourg European Court of Human Rights to revise its 1978 ruling and to declare that the five deprivation techniques amounted to torture. In 2018, the European Court of Human Rights, on procedural grounds, declined to reverse its 1978 decision. However, in late 2017, the British High Court had ruled that the failure by the Police Service of Northern Ireland (PSNI) to investigate the allegations of torture was unlawful and should be quashed. The PSNI appealed this decision to the Court of Appeal. In September 2019, the Court of Appeal confirmed the decision of the High Court. An appeal by the PSNI to the UK Supreme Court was rejected in November 2019, and in December 2021 the UK Supreme Court stated that the PSNI acted unlawfully by deciding not to proceed with an investigation into the torture of the 14 Hooded Men. Consequently, in June 2023, the PSNI issued the following apology to the internees who were subjected to the five deprivation techniques in 1971: 'The Police Service of Northern Ireland acknowledges the finding of the United Kingdom Supreme Court that it is likely that the treatment to which you and the other Hooded Men were subjected at the hands of security forces, including some police officers, would be characterised today as torture'.[2] Amazingly, it took more than fifty years to vindicate Graham Greene's concerns as expressed in his letter published by *The Times* in November 1971.

2   Irishcentral.com/news/hooded-men-apology.

Having read it, I immediately wrote to praise him, but before he even received my letter, I found myself face to face with Graham in our communal basement, both with dustbins in hand. I congratulated him warmly on his letter to *The Times*. We had a long friendly chat on the stairs. Graham was surprised to find a young Frenchman not only capable of speaking English fluently, but also apparently well versed in Irish history and politics. He invited me in for a drink in his apartment on the fourth floor of the Résidence des Fleurs. Thus began a warm friendship that lasted until his death in 1991.

From then on, we met two or three times a month in our respective apartments, and later at the Villa Dinah in the Parc Saramartel, at Les Chênes Verts on the Boulevard J. F. Kennedy in the Cap d'Antibes, the family house where we moved in 1983, but also at the Auberge Provençale on the Place Nationale, or Chez Félix, the restaurant on the harbour where Graham and Yvonne Cloetta had lunch practically every day. We enjoyed long discussions on Henry James, Joseph Conrad, Ford Madox Ford, François Mauriac, Georges Bernanos, G. K. Chesterton, and Norman Douglas, who were among his favourite writers.

An Encounter in Antibes

Graham Greene taking his breakfast on the terrace of his flat on the fourth floor of the Résidence des Fleurs overlooking the harbour of Antibes and the Fort Carré.

We often discussed the dissolution of the USSR and Gorbachev's efforts to reform his crumbling state by eliminating totalitarian aspects of the Soviet regime. Graham believed strongly that Communism in Russia would be overthrown by the KGB: its members had the brightest minds, were the cleverest and most educated people, fluent in foreign languages and familiar with the western world countries where they were posted. He was convinced that the KGB were agents of change implanted at the very heart of the Soviet regime. I sometimes wonder how he would have reacted to the invasion of Ukraine by Russian president and former intelligence officer of the KGB, Vladimir Putin.

After *perestroika* and *glasnost*, Graham felt a strong urge to revisit Russia after twenty-five years of absence. He accepted an invitation from the Writer's Union in 1985, and, in September 1986, he made a long journey with Yvonne Cloetta to Moscow, Georgia, the Black Sea, Siberia and other places. In Moscow, the couple visited Kim Philby, Graham's friend and former colleague in the Secret Intelligence Service, who had defected to Russia on 23 January 1963 shortly before being sensationally outed as a Soviet spy. I wrote a *verbatim* record of my conversation with Graham about this visit.

It was at *Chez Félix* on 15 December 1986 that Graham told me about his meeting with Philby. On the front page, I scribbled the words 'strictly confidential' as the author of *The Human Factor* did not want to find any newspaper articles on what he regarded as a strictly private visit. In revealing them now, I do not feel that I am betraying any obligation, as both Rufina Philby and Yvonne Cloetta have recounted these events in detail in their respective books.[3] Graham was asked if he wished to visit Philby. His answer was forthright: 'He knows I am here. Therefore, if he wants to see me, he will have to make the first move'. Kim Philby and his wife Rufina sent an invitation to dinner that was forwarded to Graham and Yvonne. Graham accepted on condition that the meeting would be private and that there would be no witness. Graham was anxious to meet his old mentor, but he became ever more hesitant as the time grew closer. 'He was intimidated', said Yvonne. A nervous Graham rang the apartment bell and Philby opened the door. They stared at each other, ill at ease. Philby broke the silence: 'Well, it is obvious that a lot of water has flowed by', and he added immediately, 'Please Graham, don't ask me any questions about the past.' The evening was spent discussing trivialities. But Graham could see, however, that Kim had not gone native but was still the quintessential Englishman that he had always been.

The next day, they met again. Yvonne remarked to Philby that he looked quite tired. He confessed that he had not slept at all the previous night. 'Having the opportunity to meet a friend like Graham whom I had not seen for over twenty years, how could I possibly sleep', he said.

'Is it true', I asked Graham, 'that he missed England and the English way of life'? Graham answered that he could not be certain. 'He seems

---

3   Rufina Philby, *The Private Life of Kim Philby: The Moscow Years* (London: Little Browne and Company, 1999); Yvonne Cloetta, *In Search of a Beginning: My Life with Graham Greene* (London: Bloomsbury, 2004).

to be happy in Moscow. He has married Rufina, a Russian woman younger than he is. She is very devoted to him. She has succeeded in making him smoke and drink less. A great performance, as he was a heavy drinker in the past, which was very bad for his emphysema. But during our visit to Moscow, there were no restrictions as far as the drinks were concerned. Vodka flowed in abundance during the three days we saw each other.'

'Do you think that he is still active in the KGB?' I asked. 'I don't know', said Graham. 'He may have played a role of adviser under the reign of Andropov. Under Gorbachev, it is difficult to guess if he is still operational or not. Whatever may be the case, he has no regrets.' The miserable Moscow life of the Soviet mole Maurice Castle in *The Human Factor* (1978), shows that Graham had serious doubts about Philby, likely dismissed as a spent force and sidelined by his KGB handlers.

I once asked Graham what he would have done if he had discovered before his defection that Philby was spying for the Russians. He answered instantly: 'I would have given him twenty-four hours and then I would have denounced him.' He compared Philby to an English Catholic spying for Spain in the reign of Elizabeth I, adding: 'He betrayed his country, but who among us has not committed treason to someone or something more important than a country.'

Graham Greene and Suzanne Joannon, Les Chênes Verts, Cap d'Antibes, 27 September 1980.

Ways of Escape

On the fourth floor of the Résidence des Fleurs, Graham Greene often reminisced about his earlier wanderings in Mexico, Haiti, Cuba, Paraguay and Argentina. He spoke with surprising warmth of his friendship with Omar Torrijos, ruler of Panama, and the unexpected invitation that he received from him in 1976. From then on, he visited Panama practically every year. He was proud to have been given a Panamanian passport to join the Panama delegation that signed the agreement on 7 September 1977, formally known as the Treaty Concerning the Permanent Neutrality and Operation of the Panama Canal.

I reminded him that a similar agreement had been signed between Ireland and Britain on 25 April 1938 to terminate the trade war between the two islands. It also restored immediate Irish control of the naval bases retained by the British Admiralty in accordance with the 1921 Treaty. At that time, Éamon de Valera played the role of Omar Torrijos, while Neville Chamberlain performed the part of Jimmy Carter, with Winston Churchill growling in the background. The Anglo-Irish agreement could have been equally labelled the 'Neutrality Treaty', another popular name of the treaty on the Panama Canal, as it enabled Ireland to remain neutral during World War II. Graham was amused by the parallel. He laughed heartily, adding: 'You have become more Irish than the Irish themselves.'

He followed closely the situation in Nicaragua, Central and Latin America. He smiled when I told him that, while in Haiti, we made our pilgrimage to the Hotel Oloffson, guided there by none other than Aubelin Jolicoeur, on whom he modelled the prying journalist and police informer, Petit Pierre, in his 1966 novel *The Comedians*.

On South–East Asia, I took great care to record precisely what he confessed to me: 'I took a great interest in Vietnam where I spent longer spells than in Central America. At the time of the French war, I came back two months every winter for about four years running. In Vietnam, I had a sympathy, in a sense, for both sides. I was able to see Hô Chi Minh in

Hanoi, and, as an ex-colonialist, I had a certain sympathy with the French which I didn't have later with the Americans who had come from so far away and who had no knowledge of the country. At least the French knew what they were fighting for.'

In *Ways of Escape*, he insisted on his 'ambivalent attitude to the war, already perceptible – my admiration for the French army, my admiration for their enemies, and my doubt of any final value in the war'.[1] On his fourth and last visit to Indo-China, in 1955, after the setbacks of the French in the north, he had not changed his mind: 'I was feeling ill and tired and depressed. I sympathized with the victors, but I sympathized with the French too'.[2]

I told him that my close friend Erwan Bergot was stationed in the garrison of Diên Biên Phu where he was in charge of a section of mortars during the siege of the entrenched camp. Surviving the misery of the Viet Minh internment camps, he resumed his military career. After having suffered a serious injury, he had settled down as a writer and historian of France's many wars – successful and unsuccessful. I left some of Erwan's book at the Résidence des Fleurs, notably *Deuxième classe à Dien Bien Phu* and *Les héros oubliés*, both devoted to Indo-China which Graham had called 'France's Crown of Thorns' in a notorious article of 1952.[3]

Having browsed these books, Greene reminisced about his journeys to Saigon, Hanoi, Nam Dinh and all the places which he had visited as a journalist in the fifties. He stressed that his visits were not as a secret agent, as some French intelligence officers claimed.

On his first visit in 1951, Graham had been warmly befriended by General de Lattre de Tassigny, the recently appointed commander in chief of the French forces in Indo-China. A mere eight months later, when Graham came back, the situation had deteriorated. De Lattre, who had lost his only son, had become very suspicious. The British Consul, Trevor Wilson, suspected of being an MI6 implant tasked with subverting the French war

1   Graham Greene, *Ways of Escape* (Toronto: Lester and Orpen Dennys, 1980), 133–4.
2   Greene, *Ways of Escape*, 141.
3   Graham Greene, 'Indo-China: France's Crown of Thorns', *Paris Match*, 12 July 1952; Graham Greene, *Reflections*, selected and introduced by Judith Adamson (London: Reinhardt Books, 1990), 129.

effort, was expelled. Placed under the supervision of the Sûreté, Graham Greene, Wilson's close friend and himself a former member of the SIS, expected to suffer the same fate. He pleaded with General de Lattre who remained sceptical, then with General Raoul Salan, Vice-commander of the French army who succeeded de Lattre the following year. I have obtained from the Association des Amis de Raoul Salan a copy of the letter sent from Hanoi by Graham to General Salan on 23 November 1951. This letter has escaped the attention of Greene's many biographers.

> Dear General Salan,
>
> This morning you were kind enough to invite me to put my difficulties here before you in writing.
>
> As you know I have come to Indo-China as a correspondent of *Life* (I attach a letter from their London office). During the past year *Life* has commissioned me to write a number of articles for them on Catholic subjects or on subjects which have a Catholic angle. Of these articles, they have already printed the following:
>
> 1. The Doctrine of the Assumption,
> 2. The Career of Pius XII
> 3. Malaya: The Unknown War.
>
> After the appearance of the third article, *Life* invited me to do a report of a similar character on the war in Indo-China, and they guaranteed me a minimum payment of $4,000 (I mention this figure because the smaller figure of $400 has been spoken of and regarded as a suspicious circumstance).
>
> I had hoped that as a writer well known to be a friend of France I should be trusted to present to the American people a fair picture of your struggle against Communism in the Far East. Indeed I was even presumptuous enough to hope that I might be of some service to France in helping to convey to America the vital importance of the war here. My article on Malaya was regarded by the authorities as a useful one.
>
> It is disappointing therefore to find myself regarded by the authorities here not as a friendly writer but as an intelligence agent, on no better ground than my personal friendship with Mr Trevor Wilson, the former British Consul. I would like to repeat to you what I said to General de Lattre: I am attached to no intelligence service and I have no mission here whatever except that of a writer for *Life*.
>
> To a writer, actual experience is of greater value than personal security. I am not concerned with news but with the ambience of war. The authorities in Malaya recognised that fact and allowed me to attach myself to the Gurkhas and take part in actual

operations. I hoped to be allowed also here to share in a small way in the day-to-day dangers of your troops, for example to accompany a military or maritime operation of *nettoyage*[4] and to stay in one of your more isolated posts for a long enough period to appreciate the strain that such a war necessitates.

But you will appreciate that if I am an object of suspicion to the authorities this kind of writing becomes impossible. Under these circumstances I can see no alternative but to telegraph to Mr Luce that it has become impossible for me to carry out my assignment here because of suspicions which you will forgive me thinking absurd.

I would like to add that throughout I have been treated with great courtesy. I have no complaint whatever on that score. I very much appreciate too your patience in listening to my case.

Yours sincerely
Graham Greene

Three days later, General Salan interviewed Trevor Wilson and Graham Greene and sent a factual report to Paris. I have studied this report in the archives of General Salan in the Service Historique de la Défense (SHD). Following this enquiry, and the recommendation of the General, Graham was allowed to remain in the country and to rove about freely. Greene and Salan became friends and Graham told me that he often went with the Mandarin (nickname of Salan) to smoke in opium *fumeries* in Hanoi and Saigon. Of these episodes, Greene retained the happiest memories. The two men stayed in touch over the years. Their friendship resurfaced in 1980 when Graham waged his last war against corruption and injustice in the Nice area.

During our conversations on the French war in Indo-China, I was struck by the equanimity and fairness of his complex attitude towards the protagonists who had been fighting on the ground there. He had a natural empathy for the Viet Minh and never doubted that they would win in the end, but this feeling was combined with a sincere admiration for the stubborn and even heroic stand of the French army and for the resilience of Catholic fortified enclaves like the one organised by a 30-year-old, half-French, half-Annamite, French officer, Colonel Jean Leroy, considered as the uncrowned king of Bentré in the Mekong Delta. 'He read de Tocqueville

---

4   Cleansing or clean-up.

and struck, with the suddenness and cruelty of a tiger, at the Communists in his region. I was glad years later to write a preface to his autobiography in which he did not attempt to hide the tiger's face behind the smile – a rather small return since he had probably saved my life'.[5]

At a personal level for Greene, war was an antidote to the boredom and depression as he was often tired of peaceful atmosphere with no hope of a bullet; war was always a riveting occurrence because the proximity of death revealed a man's real character; but equally it generated revulsion for the senseless violence and degrading squalor attached to it. These mixed feelings were aggravated by the ever-present guilt of being an 'old voyeur at his tricks again' and not an active participant in the fighting on the RC4,[6] in the paddy fields or in Phat Diem. Greene had no illusions about the outcome nor its consequences: he knew that the victory of Viet Minh would not open the gateway of a paradise of milk and honey. Graham wrote in *The Sunday Times* in late March 1954: 'I do not believe that ever again will one see the strange sunsets falling on the Baie d'Along, the lamp glowing on the cook's face as he prepares the opium pipe. The last performance has begun: a country one has loved is about to retire behind the curtain'.[7]

This obituary notice by a left-wing intellectual is remarkable in its sincerity: 'When everything is considered, it represents for France the end of an empire. The United States is exaggeratedly distrustful of empires, but we Europeans retain the memory of what we owe to Rome, just as Latin America knows what it owes to Spain. When the hour of evacuation sounds there will be many Vietnamese who will regret the loss of the language which put them in contact with the art and faith of the West. The injustices committed by men who were harassed, exhausted and ignorant will be forgotten and the names of a good number of Frenchmen, priests, soldiers and administrators, will remain engraved in the memory of the

---

5   Greene, *Ways of Escape*, 132; and Colonel Jean Leroy, *Fils de la Rizière*, Préface de Graham Greene (Paris: Robert Laffont, 1977).
6   RC4, acronym for Route Coloniale n°4.
7   Graham Greene, 'Last Cards in Indo-China', *Sunday Times*, 28 March 1954, reproduced in Greene *Reflections*, 172.

Vietnamese: a fort, a road intersection, a dilapidated church. "Do you remember", someone will say, "the days before the Legion left?".[8]

Twenty-six years after the fall of Diên Biên Phu, Greene summed up his nostalgia for a world in its final dissolution: 'In Indo-China I drained a magic potion, a loving-cup which I have shared since with many retired *colons* and officers of the Foreign Legion whose eyes light up at the mention of Saigon and Hanoi.'[9]

8   Greene, *Reflections*, 146–7.
9   Greene, *Ways of Escape*, 131.

A Stroll in Ireland after the Civil War

One should not think that we were always talking. Often, we sipped our drinks quietly, happy to be together. I introduced him to 12-year-old Jameson Irish whiskey for which he developed a taste, recalling that Jameson was the favourite brand of his lover Catherine Walston. He shared his lethal recipe for extra dry martinis: 'Put some Noilly Prat with ice cubes in a glass, stir for thirty seconds, then empty the vermouth and ice, and fill the frozen glass right to the brim with gin.' Graham once invited me to drink miniature bottles of vodka and aquavit given to him on a Scandinavian airline. He smiled when I said that we were like James Wormold and Captain Segura in *Our Man in Havana*. I stopped before falling asleep like the Cuban army officer in the novel.

I asked Graham if I could interview him on Ireland, his life in the South of France and other subjects. Even though he was notoriously hostile to any form of interviews, he spontaneously accepted, and he may even have enjoyed the experience. A long interview entitled 'Graham Greene's Other Island' was eventually published in the December 1981 issue of the scholarly journal *Etudes Irlandaises*, of which I was then editor. It was reissued in the *Irish Press* on 26 March 1982, in the *Irish Independent* on 1 July 1989, and in two collections of articles published in the United States: *Conversations with Graham Greene* (1992) and *Graham Greene, Man of Paradox* (1994).

Even though the Irish censor banned four of his books,[1] he remained extremely fond of Ireland. The connection went back a long way. At 16, towards the end of the Irish War of Independence, while he attended the Berkhamsted School of which his father was headmaster, he had whole-heartedly supported a debating resolution stating 'That in the opinion of this House the Government's policy of reprisals in Ireland is unjustifiable'.

---

1 The Irish Censorship Board banned *The Heart of the Matter, The End of the Affair, England Made Me* and *The Quiet American*. Michael Adams, *Censorship: The Irish Experience* (Dublin: Scepter Press, 1968), 250.

He was barely 18 years old when he walked with a cousin from Dublin to Waterford. The Irish Civil War had just ended and the scars left from the struggle left a lasting memory on the young writer's mind. He described his wanderings in the *Weekly Westminster Gazette* of 25 August 1923. This early piece of patronising journalism revealed that acute sense of observation that would be the hallmark of his later writings. Here he describes his first encounter with the Irish predicament:

> As the train moved out of Kingstown for Dublin, my first feeling was that here was the Ireland of the Irish Players [Abbey Theatre], the traditional comic Ireland. The carriage was full. A farm girl and her 'boy', a mother with two small children, an elderly couple, an unattached female, and an old gentleman with a top hat and gold-rimmed eyeglasses were with us in the carriage. While we were waiting for the train to go, the mother suddenly realised that she was without her luggage, and rushed from the coach, leaving one of her children behind. The minutes passed and the child began to weep. After some time the unattached female took the boy upon her knee, where it continued to weep. Presently the guard appeared and inserted a key in the lock. After waiting to see if someone else would speak, the unattached female raised an indignant voice. 'Don't lock that door', she cried, 'a woman's gone off and left her baby here'. 'Sure', said the guard slowly, 'she wouldn't be deserting her baby It's foolish you are'. With stern dignity, and with a perfect belief in his own logical behaviour, he locked the door and departed. The child cried harder than ever and would not be comforted. The elderly man in the corner sank quietly asleep; his wife made a tentative effort to silent the boy, but all was of no avail. Of a sudden I was conscious of a movement beside me. The old gentleman in the top hat was slowly stirring, like a piece of disused machinery, put into unwonted movement. I could almost hear the creaking of the parts. After a long and laborious fumbling in some deeply hidden pocket, he abstracted a dilapidated chocolate cream, and still without a word presented it to the boy. Silence reigned in the carriage.
>
> At last everything was settled comfortably, as in a popular novel, and the train started. The first indications of the new Ireland occurred just outside Dublin, in the shape of a barricade, behind which was stationed a sentry, with fixed bayonet. But as soon as we left the station, all signs of a comic Ireland vanished.
>
> We were tired, our rucksacks were heavy, and we had looked forward in happy expectation to one night of comfort before our walk commenced. But when we inquired for our hotel from a passer-by, we learned that the servants were on strike and had picketed the entrance. As we had no desire to be made conspicuous, we went elsewhere, and since the hotel dinner was too expensive for our moderate means, we asked a theatre-goer the whereabouts of a moderately cheap restaurant. I dare not

name the place to which we were directed lest an action for libel should be lodged against me. In a rash moment I ordered liver and bacon. The liver was the colour of good gorgonzola cheese; I will not speak of the bacon. My language might go too far. The prices, however, were higher than the average English restaurant, and this cannot have been due, as elsewhere, to our nationality since the prices were clearly printed upon the menu.

It is the poverty and the expensiveness of Dublin that first impress visitors. The houses are dilapidated, the roads unswept. The two principal thoroughfares, Grafton Street and Sackville Street, would disgrace an English country town, and beggars are as numerous as in a continental port. Every space of blank wall is painted in scarlet or red, 'The Republic Lives', 'Up the IRA'. General Mulcahy, whose Flogging Bill is very unpopular, and Mr [Tim] Healy come in for most comment. 'Fight clean, Mulcahy, don't murder' decorates one building, while along the length of another wall runs, 'Tim Healy, traitor to both sides, swears allegiance to England. Don't be a fool, Tim, fight'.

These notices, it is true, mean very little. The greater number of them are written up at nightfall by young girls, still at the 'flapper' age, who seem at the moment to be the only active Republicans in the city, but they are the hardest with whom to deal. If they are put in jail, they hunger strike and become martyrs. Thirteen women were qualifying for this heavenly crown at the time when we were in Dublin, and the Government, though it had definitely stated that there would be no more releases, were forced to surrender Marie Camelford[2] unconditionally. A more efficacious punishment was invented by a Free State soldier, who, finding a girl engaged on this work of propaganda, quietly emptied the pot of red paint over her head, and passed on his way.

Two bodies of men are to be seen in the streets, one is the Free State army, the other the Civic Guard. The Civic Guard, many of whom are old RIC men, look smart and well disciplined, but they carry no arms, and are useless save for ordinary police routine. The specimens of the army which we saw in the capital were not encouraging. There seemed to be little discipline, only one in fifty condescended to salute an officer, if he met him in the street, and they consisted chiefly of old men and boys. One picture remains firmly fixed on my mind, that of a small boy of about 15,

---

2   Máire Comerford (1893–1982), a prominent republican, activist and journalist opposed the Anglo-Irish Treaty of 1921 and joined the Four Courts garrison. Arrested several times in 1923, she staged two hunger strikes, one in Mountjoy Jail, the second for twenty-seven days in Kilmainham Jail. Her memoirs, written mainly in the 1940s and 1950s, were published in 2021 by Lilliput Press in Dublin under the title *On Dangerous Ground: A Memoir of the Irish Revolution*.

> in the green uniform of the Free State, fast asleep on a bench in St Stephen's Green, his head resting on the shoulder of a still younger girl.
>
> But the most impressive thing about Dublin is its expectant, but apathetic air. Everyone is idle, but waiting. The stark ruins of the Four Courts and the Custom House, and a silent crowd of perhaps fifty people listening to a barrel-organ, or watching an officer giving orders to a sentry, are symbols of the Dublin of today. It is like that most nightmarish of dreams, when one finds oneself in some ordinary and accustomed place, yet with a constant fear at the heart that something terrible, unknown and unpreventable is about to happen.[3]

This juvenile report reveals Greene's innate curiosity, attention to significant details and the ability to anticipate what is soon going to happen on the ground. In a good article on Ireland and 'Greeneland', Charles Duffy remarked: 'It was on this brief trip to Ireland that he first sketched the topography of the better known foreign Greeneland which was to summon him so strongly during the next seven decades. At the very least, the Irish trip shows Greene fascination with the key ingredients of his later fictional worlds: shabby streets, bombed-out buildings, military occupation, a snatch of love between a soldier and his girl'.[4] Graham Greene, who detested any talk of 'Greeneland', would have poured scorn on such hyperbole.

Another anecdote involving Graham and Ireland is recounted by Ronald Matthews in his *Mon ami Graham Greene*, whose translation into English Greene strenuously opposed as he considered it badly written and overblown. Matthews recalled a confession to him by Graham in Oxford in the mid-20s:

> Ireland had just obtained its independence, but the six Protestant counties of the North remained under the jurisdiction of Britain. The new government of Northern Ireland was no less dissatisfied by this implementation of partition than the Dublin government of independent Ireland. There were rumours of armed men massing on both sides of the new border, the Northern loyalists to restore the Union between Ireland and Great Britain, the Southern nationalist to absorb the six counties in the new Irish Free State. On both sides, nobody knew exactly what the other side was up

---

3   Graham Greene, 'Impressions of Dublin', *Weekly Westminster Gazette*, 25 August 1923. Reproduced in Greene, *Reflections*, 14.
4   Charles Duffy, 'Ireland and Greeneland: The Irish in the Writings of Graham Greene', *Éire-Ireland*, xxx, 3 (1995), 17.

to. I saw there an opportunity to offer my services as secret agent. The border, as you can imagine, was closely monitored, and it was obvious that an Irishman wandering with an inquisitive air on the wrong side would have been vigorously told to mind his own business. Accordingly, I wrote to the Irish authorities to expose the problem. I suggested that an Oxford student would not attract attention while holidaying on the Northern side of the border and that I would be able to send regular reports on what was going on, subject, needless to say, to the reimbursement of my expenses. I think that the Irish were even more cautious than the Germans had been. No emissary of the Irish government came knocking at my door. There was not even a period of silence during which I could have dreamt at that new assignment. They answered quasi immediately that the border was not so tight as one was led to believe, that they already had precise information on what was going on, and that they didn't need my obliging services.[5]

I once asked Graham if this story was accurate. Amused by my discovery, he confirmed every word. We raised our glasses to his failed career of secret agent for the Irish Free State. In a more orthodox fashion, he later joined the British Intelligence Service: many are convinced that he never ceased to belong to it for the rest of his long life. We never spoke directly about it as I knew from experience that Graham, on such a subject, followed the wise Irish adage: 'Whatever you say, say nothing'.

---

5   Ronald Matthews, *Mon Ami Graham Greene* (Paris: Desclée de Brouwer, 1957), 88–89.

An Idyll in Achill

Early in 1947, feeling depressed and restless, Graham Greene started contemplating escaping from England. He wanted badly to disappear like Ambrose Bierce in Mexico, Rimbaud in Abyssinia or Gauguin in the South Seas. His friends were aware of his desperate thirst for expatriation. Evelyn Waugh wrote to him about it: 'Who on earth', answered Graham, 'told you I was going to Kenya? It was probably a half-hearted melancholy joke. I should like to compromise and go to Ireland because I like the Irish and approve so strongly of their recent neutrality, but Vivienne has an anti-Irish phobia, so I can never do that'.[1]

This was a poor excuse. His marriage had failed due to his inability to commit to a stable married life. He knew that it was his fault and confessed it bluntly to his wife Vivienne: 'We have lived for years too far from reality, and the fact that has to be faced, dear, is that by my nature, my selfishness, even in some degree by my profession, I should always, and with anyone, have been a bad husband. I think, you see, my restlessness, moods, melancholia, even my outside relationships, are symptoms of a disease and not the disease itself, and the disease, which has been going on ever since my childhood and was only temporarily alleviated by psycho-analysis, lies in a character profoundly antagonistic to ordinary domestic life. Unfortunately the disease is also one's material. Cure the disease and I doubt whether a writer would remain'.[2]

Yet, despite the breakdown of their marriage, Graham and Vivienne remained united by a strong bond of respect and affection all their lives. One of Greene's closest friends, Leopoldo Duran, a Catholic priest, lecturer in English literature at the University of Madrid and model for *Monsignore Quixote,* argued that 'it was his marriage, bound as it was for disaster, which

---

[1] Richard Greene, ed., *Graham Greene: A Life in Letters* (London: Little Brown, 2007), 139.
[2] Greene, *Graham Greene: A Life in Letters*, 159.

was the cause of Graham becoming the great writer he was. I mean the writer who decided to make theology the backbone of virtually everything he wrote. Thanks to Vivienne, Graham became a convert to Catholicism. Vivienne was the channel for grace'.[3]

At the time, however, in the winter of 1946, he had already met the flamboyant woman who would be the consuming passion of his life for the next thirteen years and who would also connect him to Ireland. Catherine Walston was the American wife of the British millionaire Lord Henry (Harry) Walston (Baron Walston), the mother of small children, and aged 30 to Greene's 43 when they met. She was beautiful, clever, rich, sexy, uninhibited and 'unhaunted by guilt' like Sarah in *The End of the Affair*. Willing to turn Catholic, she had asked Graham to be her godfather since his books had inspired her strong desire to convert. They immediately fell in love, consummating their passionate relationship in remote Dooagh on Achill Island, in the West of Ireland, where Catherine Walston had a little fisherman's stone cottage with a corrugated roof, no electricity and an outside tap for water.

They spent April 1947 on Achill. When Greene returned to England, it become quite evident that Ireland had fundamentally transformed him. In a letter to Catherine, he wrote: 'Oh hell, darling. Achill looks like being the only good thing in 1947.'[4] His burning desire was to return as quickly as possible to their remote idyll on the wild Mayo coast. On 27 June 1947, he scribbled a few words to his lover from his office in Eyre and Spottiswoode: 'This is just a note to pursue you as quickly as possible to Achill and to remind you of three things – that I'm still terribly in love with you, that I miss you (your voice saying "Good morning, Graham" at tea time), and that I want you. I want to be filling the turf buckets for you and sitting next door working, hearing the clank of washing-up, and your whistle and I want to help you make lunch.'[5] Longing for this life of simplicity animated by passionate love on the shores of the Atlantic, he sleepwalked to the Café Royal and downed a pint of beer while reading *The*

[3] Leopoldo Duran, *Graham Greene Friend and Brother* (London: Harper Collins, 1994), 315.
[4] Greene, *Graham Greene: A Life in Letters*, 141.
[5] Greene, *Graham Greene: A Life in Letters*, 143.

Aran Islands by John Millington Synge. He cannot wait: 'I want to begin the next book with you in Ireland – if possible at Achill, but on Aran or Inishbofin or the Galway hotel or anywhere.'[6]

Achill, to which the couple would retreat whenever possible, remained a hugely resonant place for Graham Greene, where his most passionate love affair flamed, but also the hidden location that he associated with his discovery of a new way of life stripped down to its bare essentials, the 'opening of a door' as he put it. That Achill door brought him an intensity of love and passion, but equally obsession, jealously, guilt and despair. Achill Island allowed Greene to cut himself off from the artificial and superficial literary London, from his family and his mistress of the war years, and from Catherine Walston's husband, children and circle of rich friends. It fired his creative imagination, allowing him to work on *The Heart of the Matter* and *Fallen Idol*, and to begin his magnificent novel *The End of the Affair*.

Greene was so taken with Achill Island and the surrounding area that he even considered relinquishing writing, marrying Catherine and purchasing a country hotel, The Old Head at Killsallagh near Louisburgh, on the south side of Clew Bay. It proved a passing fancy: Graham's real desire was the fulfilment of his passionate love affair rather than fully immersing himself in Irish life.

In 1949, to mark the second anniversary of his smouldering relationship with Catherine, Graham produced *After Two Years*. It was a tiny booklet of poems and its twenty-five copies were published privately in Capri.

> *In a plane your hair was blown,*
> *And in an island the old car*
> *Lingered from inn to inn,*
> *Like a fly on a map.*
> *A mattress was spread on a cottage floor*
> *And a door closed on a world, but another door*
> *Opened, and I was far*
> *From the old world sadly known*
> *Where the fruitless seeds were sown*
> *And they called that virtue and this sin.*
> *Did I ever love God before I knew the place*

---

6   Greene, *Graham Greene: A Life in Letters*, 146.

> *I rest in now, now with my hand*
> *Set in stone, never to move?*
> *For this is love, and this I love,*
> *And even my God is here.*[7]

On Achill, Greene became a close friend of Ernie O'Malley who was living nearby in Burrishoole Lodge, an eight-bedroom stone house situated between Achill and Mulranny on the northern shore of Clew Bay. O'Malley had been commander of the Second Southern Division of the IRA during the War of Independence, and later assistant Chief of Staff, with the rank of general, in the anti-Treaty IRA during the Civil War. Severely injured and consigned to Mountjoy Jail under sentence of death, he was eventually released for medical reasons in July 1924. Bitter and disenchanted, he left Ireland and wandered for several years on the continent and in America. Moving around California, he settled in the artist's colony at Taos, New Mexico, where he mingled with the artists and writers inspired by Mabel Dodge Luhan and D. H. Lawrence. He wrote poetry and drafted the first version of his searing *On Another Man's Wound*, the only literary masterpiece to have emerged from the Irish War of Independence. He married the wealthy American sculptor Helen Hooker in 1935, returned to Ireland that same year and divided his time between Mayo and Dublin, writing about paintings and organizing exhibitions. Their extensive art collection included works by Georges Rouault, Henry Moore, Amedeo Modigliani, Jack Butler Yeats, Evie Hone, Mainie Jellett, Paul Henry, Nano Reid and John Piper.

O'Malley, who was by then separated from his wife, was feeling lonely and isolated on Achill. He found it difficult to have a conversation about books, literature or the arts, and he undoubtedly enjoyed Graham's intellectual cut and thrust. Greene must have been attracted to the disillusioned soldier and political activist who, like him, but in a more direct way, had experienced the vertiginous feeling of living on the dangerous edge of things.

---

7   Quoted by Norman Sherry, *The Life of Graham Greene, Volume II, 1939–1955* (London: Jonathan Cape, 1994), 279.

Ernie O'Malley, revolutionary turned writer and art critic, introduced Graham to the works of his friend, the painter Jack B. Yeats, brother of W. B. Yeats. Graham liked his work so much that he purchased two of them – *A horseman enters a town at night* and *Man in a room thinking*. They hung in Greene's apartment in Paris. In 2011, both paintings were auctioned by Christie's of London to a private collector for a combined total of 500,000 euros. *The Horseman* is considered to be among Yeats's finest paintings.

Graham told me an anecdote about O'Malley: 'One day in Achill, I asked him at what time high tide was. He hesitated a long time, a look of caution came into his eyes and his attitude became typical of the Old IRA man determined not to give any information to a possible enemy. "Well Graham, it all depends", he said laconically in the end.'

It has been alleged that the friendship between Graham Greene and Ernie O'Malley may also have been due to the fact that both of them were Catherine Walston's lovers.[8] On 24 June 2017, in Hodges and Figgis, Dublin's main bookstore, I met Ernie O'Malley's son, Cormac. He dismissed the shared lover story: 'There was indeed a close intellectual and family friendship from 1933 to 1957 between Ernie O'Malley and Catherine Walston, but Harry Walston would never have allowed Ernie O'Malley and me to stay in Newton Hall from 1953 to 1956 if there had been the type of relationship which has been suggested by William Cash and others. I have found in my files references of slanderous comments by my mother about Ernie, Catherine and several other women. She was confronted by Catherine Walston and Ernie O'Malley with Seebohm Rowntree and Liam Redmond as witnesses. She was threatened with legal action by Catherine Walston and backed off.'[9]

On the subject, William Cash was extremely prudent: he wrote cautiously that Catherine and Ernie were 'probably lovers and possibly continued to be so after Walston began her affair with Greene'.[10] It has also been asserted that, in the 1950s, she had affairs with a succession of clerics,

---

8   William Cash, *The Third Woman: The Secret Passion That Inspired the End of the Affair* (London: Little Brown & Company, 2000), 91.
9   Cormac O'Malley to the author, email 12 July 2017.
10 Cash, *The Third Woman*, 28.

including Father Donal O'Sullivan, the Jesuit who became the autocratic head of the Arts Council in Dublin.[11]

William Cash writes in a cavalier way at the beginning of his book: 'The lasting impact that Walston had on Greene's life and work is now indisputable. It was the wrenching drama of Greene's tortured, guilt-ridden affair with Walston that provided the basis for the moral and religious dilemmas faced by the major characters in many of his books, from *The Heart of the Matter* (1948) to *A Burnt-Out Case* (1961), including *The Quiet American* (1955), *Our Man in Havana* (1958), the screenplays of *The Fallen Idol* (1948) and *The Third Man* (1949) and his most successful plays, *The Living Room* (1953) and *The Complaisant Lover* (1959). After Greene's affair with Walston finally ended, his creativity never fully recovered. Neither did his Catholic faith.'[12] Cash asserted that the collapse of the affair hollowed out one of the most successful writers of the twentieth century to 'a creative husk'.[13] However, Greene was far from a spent force after 1960: consider *Travels with my Aunt* (1969), *The Honorary Consul* (1973), *The Human Factor* (1978), and the hilarious *Monsignor Quixote* (1982).

To overemphasize the influence of Catherine Walston on Graham's life and works seems as reductive and misleading as the crucial role attributed to Vivienne by Father Leopoldo Duran. Graham and Vivienne's marriage lasted twenty years, the affair with Catherine Walston lasted thirteen years, but the relationship between Graham and Yvonne Cloetta lasted thirty years. One should not underestimate the influence of Yvonne – a sweet tiny blonde brimful of charm, wit, and energy. One had only to share a lunch or spend an afternoon with Yvonne and Graham to know that they were united by a bond of trusting and caring love. Yvonne gave Graham something that he had never experienced before her: peace and tranquillity. The Graham Greene that I knew was a man reconciled with himself, purged of the insecurity and boredom of earlier years. Ian Thomson in his introduction to *Articles of Faith* provided an accurate judgement of Yvonne's

11 John Banville, *Timepieces: A Dublin Memoir* (London: Hachette Books, 2016) 10; Pat Cooke, *The Politics and Polemics of Culture in Ireland 1800–2010* (London: Routledge, 2021).
12 Cash, *The Third Woman*, 28.
13 Cash, *The Third Woman*, 28.

calming influence: 'Cloetta eased the writer through his brooding introspection, and became his lifelong counsellor and confidante. She oversaw French translations of Greene's books, suggested titles for them and even edited the journal he kept of his dreams, *A World of My Own*, published posthumously in 1992. Cloetta was effectively Greene's life partner; indeed he was furious when she was described in the 1989 *Tablet* interview as his "girlfriend". "How could I possibly refer to somebody I have known for thirty years as a girlfriend?" Greene complained.'[14]

The claim that Graham discarded his Catholicism after having parted with Catherine Walston is also dubious. Graham had always been an eccentric Catholic to say the least. A limerick in *Punch* in 1982 pokes fun at his peculiar brand of religious persuasion:

> *The crankiest Christian that ever was seen*
> *Is surely His Eminence Graham Greene.*
> *His creatures find scandal and degradation*
> *The sole sure means to attain salvation.*[15]

In the early fifties, at the beginning of his affair with Catherine, he opined that 'the vision of faith as an untroubled sea was lost for ever; faith was more like a tempest in which the lucky were engulfed and lost, and the unfortunate survived to be flung battered and bleeding on the shore. A better man could have found a life's work on the margin of that cruel sea.'[16] Graham lived and loved on the shore of that cruel sea throughout his life. He was never a pious craw thumping Christian; his life was always intemperate; and he was often at loggerheads with the Papacy. For him, the dogma of papal infallibility was insane and ridiculous; sin never formed part of his vocabulary; and he did not believe in Hell. However, he regularly attended Mass in Antibes; he enjoyed the company of priests and clerics, particularly Jesuits; and he carried a picture of Padre Pio in his wallet. On the shelves of his library in the Résidence des Fleurs, he showed me several treatises on theology, adding: 'Theology is the only form of

---

14 Ian Thomson, ed., *Articles of Faith: The Collected Tablet Journalism of Graham Greene* (Oxford: Signal Books, 2006), xix.
15 Thomson, *Articles of Faith*, xii.
16 Greene, *Ways of Escape*, 217.

philosophy which I enjoy reading'. On many occasions, he described himself as 'a Catholic agnostic', a perfect oxymoron. Graham was a tormented Catholic who discarded rigid dogma but who retained his spiritual orientation to the very end. In old age, he returned to the sacraments and he received the last rites on his deathbed. Endowed with an unorthodox but deep sense of spirituality, he was a man 'in search of a beginning'.

A Most Peculiar Relationship

In his autobiography, Sean O'Faolain recalls his encounter with Graham Greene in 1947. Like Ernie O'Malley, O'Faolain had been in the IRA during the War of Independence and on the anti-Treaty side during the Civil War. Disillusioned by the disappointing narrow state that he had fought to liberate as a young revolutionary, he spent some years in America, mostly in Harvard where he was a Commonwealth Fellow and then a Harvard Fellow. Later he taught at St Mary's College, at Strawberry Hill, in London, before returning to Ireland in 1933. As a public intellectual, short-story writer, novelist, biographer and essayist, he was the key activist in Ireland's cultural life, a world demoralised by a rigid and stifling censorship. In 1941, he founded *The Bell*, a monthly journal which stimulated debate designed to ruffle the complacent consciences that had been dulled by what was in essence a clericalist Free State.

In London, Sean O'Faolain received a message in 1947 from the publishing company Eyre and Spottiswoode that Graham Greene wanted to speak with him: 'I had met Graham only once before, in Dublin, accompanied by a very beautiful young woman, very volatile, very vivacious (…) I had been taken by his relaxed, boyish, devil-may-care style, surprisingly different to his grim novels, films and plays'.[1] O'Faolain arranged to meet with Greene the next day at one o'clock in the publisher's premises.

When he turned up, he was directed to an empty room in which he was soon joined by the same beautiful woman that he had met in Dublin. She looked like a female character in a novel by Evelyn Waugh, Virginia Woolf, or PG Wodehouse. Sitting behind the desk, 'she began the sort of chat that women who are aware of their attractions pour out like champagne after the cork has hit the ceiling, a gift I envy but cannot emulate

---

1   Sean O'Faolain, *Vive Moi! An Autobiography* (London: Sinclair Stevenson, 1993), 333.

being the reserved sort of chap who can only froth after his third Martini'.[2] Trying to arouse the reserved Irishman, 'she whirled her chair at right angles to me, stretched out from behind the desk her crossed legs (absolute Greek perfection), glanced at my still orientally impassive eyes, snorted "I don't believe you are interested in girls at all" and in silence started to read Graham's correspondence'.[3] O'Faolain, who was actually a man of serial affairs, including one with the novelist Elizabeth Bowen, later thought that the two had had a bet as to whether she would succeed in titillating him. He wondered if Greene did this with all his authors, or only with Catholic ones.

Julia O'Faolain, Sean's daughter, suggested that Graham intentionally left him alone with the girl to see if she could seduce him, and asked 'Is Graham Greene a voyeur? And Sean a guinea pig?'.[4] More likely, it was an illustration of Greene's uncontrollable love of practical jokes.

Graham eventually appeared and led everybody to a nearby French restaurant where the Martinis and wine eased the tense atmosphere, especially so when Greene made an unexpected proposal to O'Faolain that he write a book for Eyre and Spottiswoode. Sean queried what kind of book was envisaged and was surprised when Greene suggested a travel book:

- The last travel book I wrote was about Ireland and it got me into no end of trouble with an Irish bishop! A crude creature, but powerful.
- Well this time write about some place where bishops however crude are not powerful. Say Italy?
- I have never been to Italy!
- Then go there.
- I have no money.
- I will give you £500 in advance of future royalties in exchange for a travel book on Italy.[5]

2   O'Faolain, *Vive Moi!*, 333.
3   O'Faolain, *Vive Moi!*, 333.
4   Julia O'Faolain, *Trespassers: A Memoir* (London: Faber and Faber, 2013), 102.
5   O'Faolain, *Vive Moi!*, 333.

£500 was then a considerable sum. O'Faolain was stunned: 'Here I was suddenly invited by Graham Greene to share in and to describe the lifeways and the traditions of one of the most civilized countries in history.'[6] This invitation came at the right time, as O'Faolain was impatient to explore new ground, 'having grown a little wary of abusing our bourgeoisie, Little Irelanders, chauvinists, puritans, stuffed-shirts, pietists, Tartuffes, Anglophobes, Celtophiles, et *alii hujus generis*'.[7]

He instantly accepted the generous offer and his explorations provided him with material for two travel books – *A Summer in Italy* and *An Autumn in Italy*. These were the books that he himself most cherished because in them he felt free to express himself completely unbridled as an artist for the first time. Freed from the narrow ground of Ireland, O'Faolain's encounter with Italy allowed him to contemplate a wider version of human nature. He always remained grateful for Greene's generosity.

He was more reticent about the Englishman's attitude to life and his peculiar brand of faith. In the spring of 1953, O'Faolain accepted an invitation to deliver six lectures at Princeton University as part of the Christian Gauss Seminars in Criticism. His theme was to explore what marked off modern literature from its predecessors by examining prominent writers of the 'fervent twenties'.

His Princeton audiences in the Firestone Library were so enthralled that he was encouraged to publish his lectures. *The Vanishing Hero: Studies in Novelists of the Twenties* was published in London by Eyre and Spottiswoode in 1956. O'Faolain covered Aldous Huxley, Evelyn Waugh, Graham Greene, William Faulkner, Ernest Hemingway, Virginia Woolf and two Irish novelists – Elizabeth Bowen and James Joyce.

O'Faolain detected extremism in Graham Greene's novels, particularly in *The Heart of the Matter*, taking an idea to the limits of its implications but with the consequence of dehumanising his characters: 'His obsession with the ugly and evil side of life is equally troubling. More than occasionally, one feels that he is not merely outraging nature but that he is taking a perverse

---

6   O'Faolain, *Vive Moi!*, 304.
7   Sean O'Faolain, 'Signing off', *The Bell*, xii, April 1946.

pleasure in rubbing its face in its own ordure.'[8] Greene's description of the hideous town in *The Lawless Roads* reminds him of Joyce's devastatingly bleak representations of Dublin at its most dreary. The persistent theme of Greene's novels is betrayal and treason. His attitude to life transgresses the borderline of the morbid and corrupt. And Greene's faith is highly questionable: 'Evil and ugliness inspire him. They are the compost of his flower-garden. Faith, for him, is not a gift, it is won from Despair. Love relies on the validity of Hate.'[9]

O'Faolain accuses Graham of being a covert Jansenist, linking him to a motley crew including 'the ascetically minded Catholic, the natural sceptic with no interest in religion, the soured hedonist, the frustrated romantic, the earnest social reformer, the topical satirist. The list of candidates for the title of neo-Pascalians in our time is long: Bernanos, Julien Green, Mauriac, Céline, Marcel Aymé, Camus, Faulkner, Moravia, George Orwell, Graham Greene – all of them anti-humanist, anti-heroic, highly skeptical about man's inherent dignity which the great humanist tradition took as the cornerstone of all its beliefs'.[10] O'Faolain regards their shared misgivings about free will as the essence of Jansenism: 'The central Jansenist doctrine was that man cannot be saved by his own efforts. Alone he is helpless. He depends for salvation on the arbitrary, if not actually capricious gift of Grace which he can neither achieve of his own efforts nor, if it is granted to him, resist'.[11]

A preference for nihilism over human nature, the highly developed sense of innate evil, and the belief that only through pain does one truly discover oneself, these are vital elements in Greene's novels, mimicking the core Jansenist conviction that man, of himself, can do nothing to save himself. Only God can save the soul of the sinner: 'I suffer, therefore I am', which leads to 'I suffer, therefore I may be saved'.

O'Faolain reacted angrily to this obliteration of human freedom. He attended the 1953 premiere of Graham's play *The Living Room*: 'I left the

8   O'Faolain, *The Vanishing Hero: Studies in Novelists of the Twenties* (London: Eyre and Spottiswoode, 1956), 74.
9   O'Faolain, *The Vanishing Hero*, 74.
10 O'Faolain, *The Vanishing Hero*, 80–81.
11 O'Faolain, *The Vanishing Hero*, 81.

theatre on the first night in a state of rage which, I later recognised, must have been somewhat like the state of irritation into which the seventeenth-century Jansenists threw their Jesuit opponents – men with a sweeter conception of God's world'.[12] The Irishman told his Princeton audience: 'I have grown a little weary both of Greene's message and his methods'.[13]

Yet, O'Faolain paid tribute to Graham's 'enormous invention, his graphic eye, one of the quickest minds working in fiction today, and an inflammable and infectious imagination'.[14] He praised him in the following terms: 'Graham Greene has expanded our view of human nature by his constant insistence on divine pity and divine mercy, and he must, in doing this, have brought courage and consolation to a great number of readers.'[15]

12 O'Faolain, *The Vanishing Hero*, 90.
13 O'Faolain, *The Vanishing Hero*, 95.
14 O'Faolain, *The Vanishing Hero*, 91.
15 O'Faolain, *The Vanishing Hero*, 95.

A Foray into Northern Ireland

In 1977, Greene was invited by the Northern Ireland Office, led at the time by Merlyn Rees, to visit Belfast to study the situation in Northern Ireland first hand. Always attracted to odd places torn by conflict, internecine divisions and guerrilla wars, he accepted on condition that he would be free to travel around the Six Counties in the company of his friend Gerry Fitt, chairman of the Social Democratic and Labour Party.

Gerry Fitt had initially been a merchant seaman. From 1962 onwards he sat in the Northern Ireland parliament at Stormont as a member of the Republican Labour Party for the Dock Ward of Belfast. He was elected to Westminster as MP for West Belfast. As a staunch supporter of the Civil Rights movement, he was injured in the brutal assault on the Derry demonstration of 5 October 1968. Re-elected to Westminster in 1970, he took part in the discussions which led to the foundation of the Social Democratic and Labour Party of which he became leader. When the British government finally replaced the disgraced Stormont by an Assembly, Fitt became Deputy Chief in the short-lived power-sharing Executive of this Assembly that lasted from July 1973 until May 1974. After the catastrophic collapse of Sunningdale and the return to Direct Rule, he was deprived of the leadership of the SDLP by John Hume. Always a fierce opponent of the Provisional IRA, he was created a life peer in 1983 under the name Baron Fitt, the only nationalist or republican from Northern Ireland ever to agree to enter the House of Lords. Gerry Fitt agreed to be Graham Greene's mentor during his five-day mission in and around Belfast.

Graham told me that these five days had been among the most terrible in his life, far more frightening than Indochina, Haiti, or the Blitz. He felt exposed as an obvious target for the Provos. As an English Catholic, a known former British intelligence agent, and a high-profile guest of the Northern Ireland Office swanning around in a chauffeur-driven government car, he could be considered in that terrible phrase, 'a legitimate target', by the IRA.

Being accompanied by Gerry Fitt rubbed salt in the wound. Graham told me how, in the various Belfast pubs that they visited, Fitt kept one hand on his pint and the other on a revolver in his pocket while his security detail always sat facing the door. On one occasion, noticing that a customer had slipped out when they walked in, Fitt said: 'Let's get out of here quick: they will be here in ten minutes'.

Graham was genuinely horrified by what he heard from victims of the Troubles. 'Since I was a teenager, I had a romantic leaning towards the Old IRA of the 1920s, and the Irish struggle for independence. Today, the situation is very different. I don't see any similarity between the Provisional IRA and the Old IRA. There are no bonds between the terrorists of today and the idealists like Erskine Childers or Michael Collins who were heroes of my youth.'[1]

Interviewed in Antibes, in 1979, by Marie-Françoise Allain, daughter of his friend, a French intelligence officer assassinated in Morocco, Graham denied that the Provos were fighting a just war: 'They are not the victims. They are the executioners like the minister Reginald Maudling and his "clean torture" which made me ashamed of being English (...) The Provos have become real gangsters, devoid of ideals. One might as well be in Chicago. They are putting pressure on small shopkeepers. If they don't give in, they are subject to kneecapping and shot in the knee with a handgun. They terrorize the Catholics. They own the taxis; they own the supermarkets. They amass fortunes thanks to terrorism.'[2]

On the other hand, Greene strongly condemned murders by loyalist commandos: 'It's no longer a question of "Protestants" against "Catholics" but of two terrorist gangs.'[3] Greene loathed the antiquated bigotry of Ian Paisley and his deluded followers. He concluded that Paisley was in no danger in Belfast as the Provos considered him their best recruiting agent. Paisley's Democratic Unionist Party was certainly the most introverted,

---

1 'Graham Greene's Other Island', an interview by Pierre Joannon, *Études Irlandaises*, 1981, 6, p. 160. See Annex 1.
2 Graham Greene, *L'Autre et son Double*, Entretiens avec Marie-Françoise Allain (Paris: Pierre Belfond, 1981), 150–1.
3 Greene, *L'Autre et son Double*, 151.

reactionary and hate-filled party in the whole United Kingdom, until the advent of UKIP.

There was another reason for Graham's harrowing memories of his five days in Northern Ireland. If he escaped the bombs and the bullets, he might be exposed to the equally lethal Irish tradition of the pub crawl. Greene, a hard drinker, simply could not compete with the bottomless drinking capacity of Fitt and his freeloading cronies. Most nights the Englishman was forced to withdraw early to his bedroom.

When he left claustrophic, seething edgy Belfast for Dublin, it felt like entering a different world. The sight of girls sitting on the grass with their boyfriends in St Stephen's Green was a pure delight. And he was happy to spend an enjoyable evening with Sean O'Faolain and another hard drinking Irishman, Conor Cruise O'Brien.

'The Cruiser', a formidably intelligent writer and polemicist, broke many boundaries across his multiple lives. Diplomat, international civil servant, scholar in Ghana and in America, politician, TD between 1969 and 1977, journalist, historian, author of *States of Ireland*, a book published in 1972 which exerted a major influence on the political sphere, Minister in the 1973–1977 coalition government led by Liam Cosgrave, editor-in-chief of *The Observer* and short-lived politician in Northern Ireland, he was above all a public intellectual and the most influential figure in bringing the two nations' concept and revisionist theories out of dusty academia and into mainstream politics and the media. Cruise O'Brien, who always retained an insatiable appetite for debate, attracted huge attention in the 1970s for giving intellectual force to the argument not simply that a united Ireland was not achievable by force but that it was reckless and dangerous to seek to include in a state a substantial number of people who did not wish to belong to it.

Graham Greene and Conor Cruise O'Brien obviously had much to say to each other about the Troubles in Northern Ireland. However, Conor Cruise O'Brien had also carefully studied Greene's published novels in his first and highly influential book, *Maria Cross: Imaginative Patterns in a Group of Modern Catholic Writers* (Chatto & Windus, 1954). This stimulating study was published on both sides of the Atlantic, in New York and in London, in 1954. It was written under the pseudonym of Donat

O'Donnell as Conor Cruise O'Brien, then a rising star in the Department of Foreign Affairs in Dublin, did not want to expose himself to prickly reactions on the topic of Catholicism. A second edition was brought out by the English Catholic publishers Burns and Oates in 1963: Cruise O'Brien had by then left the Irish diplomatic service, so the book could now appear under his own name.

The purpose of *Maria Cross* was to identify 'a version of Catholicism that would be more worthy of respect, if not acceptance, than the version that had oppressed my mother and myself in Ireland after my father's death.'[4] The Catholic writers discussed were François Mauriac, Georges Bernanos, Graham Greene, Sean O'Faolain, Evelyn Waugh, Charles Péguy, Paul Claudel and Léon Bloy.

Subtitled 'the anatomy of pity', the chapter on Greene defines the concept of pity as 'an equivocal and often impure disposition.'[5] As distinct from charity or compassion, pity, according to Cruise O'Brien, is a corrupt notion that infects the heart and soul of our ailing society. Greene 'more than any of our other writers, has sensed the importance and expressed the essence of this dissolving pity. *The Heart of the Matter* is a novel about the progress of pity; it exposes, not always consciously, the complex state of mind of two of the last inhabitants of Christendom, the police officer Scobie and Mr Graham Greene.'[6]

Cruise O'Brien summarises the plot of *The Heart of the Matter*, as a history of love, exile, pain and death. He detects a foreboding theological tone. The fate of Scobie, the main character, is dominated by despair and pity, but also by something much more troubling: 'Before he kills himself, he has a dialogue with God, for whom his love is tinged with pity. Scobie is committing suicide, indeed, out of pity for God, on whom he is inflicting sacrileges (…) In the theological sense, the sense of its intent, the story of Scobie is the record of an attempt to imitate Christ. Scobie's "pity", his assumption of responsibility for all suffering, is a simulacrum of the Passion.'[7]

---

4   Conor Cruise O'Brien, *Memoir: My Life and Themes* (Dublin: Poolbeg Press, 1998), 117.
5   Conor Cruise O'Brien, *Maria Cross: Imaginative Patterns in a Group of Catholic Writers* (London: Burns & Oates, 1963), 57.
6   Cruise O'Brien, *Maria Cross*, 58.
7   Cruise O'Brien, *Maria Cross*, 75–6.

In offering 'his own damnation' to save others, including God, from pain and agony, he does what Yeats's Countess Cathleen did and what Péguy's Saint Joan aspired to do. O'Brien can forgive Yeats's romanticism and Péguy's heroine for her peculiar sanctity, but not Greene for his sacrilege, 'the sentimentality and moral juggling' of *The Heart of the Matter*.[8] He denounces the book's 'intellectual dishonesty, its ellipses of approximation and selective omissions'.[9]

O'Brien then vigorously challenged Greene for his complete disdain for political and social context. Set in the British colony of Sierra Leone, the novel simply ignores the natives and remains silent on colonial domination: 'The only non-Europeans with individual parts in the story are two Syrian black-marketeers and the complicit boy Ali, a sort of Nephew Tom. There is no tension between European and non-European, no sense of history or colonialism. In marked contrast with other modern novels on colonial life – E. M. Forster's *A Passage to India*, for example, or George Orwell's *Burmese Days* – the centre of interest is reduced and simplified to the relation between the colonists themselves.'[10]

An addendum towards the end of *Maria Cross* alludes to Greene's 1955 novel *The Quiet American*. 'The themes are those we know: guilt and innocence, loyalty and treachery, hopelessly confused in the world of appearances'.[11] But Cruise O'Brien cannot now so blithely accuse Greene of ignoring the social aspects of the war in Indo-China. He admits that *The Quiet American* does constitute a political tragedy. But it is still deficient and unsatisfactory: 'The limitation which is the novel's strength – the reporter's restriction to direct personal experience – does not allow it the full scope and complexity of a political tragedy if we think of that as involving a great mesh of many varying human purposes and decisions.' And O'Brien adds a barbed sting in the tail of his criticism: 'On a more routine political level one must add that bitter anti-Americanism, defensive discomfort about colonies and apathetic anti-Communism, part of Fowler's mental furniture, make up together a cumbrous and confusing equipment'.[12]

8   Cruise O'Brien, *Maria Cross*, 81.
9   Cruise O'Brien, *Maria Cross*, 81.
10 Cruise O'Brien, *Maria Cross*, 52.
11 Cruise O'Brien, *Maria Cross*, 249.
12 Cruise O'Brien, *Maria Cross*, 251.

Despite his misgivings, Cruise O'Brien recognised that Graham Greene was a master of his trade. '*The Quiet American* is an exciting book. It is also the best novel for many years – certainly since *The Power and the Glory* – by one of the best living English novelists'.[13]

The acerbity of O'Faolain's and Cruise O'Brien's judgements on Graham Greene's distinctive brand of Catholicism is an illustration of the chasm separating converts from Catholics by birth. It also reveals the existence of a gulf separating similarly religious-minded people on either side of the Irish Sea – Julia O'Faolain talks about 'the animosity between Irish and English Catholics'.[14] For English converts in the thirties, Catholicism was a highly personal system of belief and devotion, alien to the traditional faith of their land as well as to the strict disciplinarian religion of the nearby island. Catholicism in England, when one did not belong to an old recusant Catholic family, served as a sign of a non-conformist independence of spirit, verging on repudiation of dull mainstream Englishness. In Graham Greene's case, to become a Catholic offered a powerful psychological separation from his parents and their sedate Anglicanism, an escape from the stifling bourgeois Berkhamsted home and a disengagement from the bland and insipid established religion of the majority. Artists always like to be in the minority, so becoming a Catholic in England gifted the convert an exhilarating sense of freedom, and a satisfying sense of self-fashioning, picking and choosing one's system of religious beliefs to mirror one's experience and feelings. This 'à la carte Catholicism' appealed to Greene, allowing him to reject a dubious teaching like Papal infallibility and rigid dogma on sexuality, while retaining the aesthetically satisfying 'smells and bells' rituals, the deeply personal sense of mysticism and the intellectually satisfying heft and depth of Catholic theology. By contrast Catholicism had congealed in Ireland into an oppressive crust of conservatism and habit, replacing spirituality with mere piety and refusing any serious intellectual engagement. To be Catholic in Ireland was to be a conformist, and every artist eventually drowned under the dead weight of an inescapable sea of social pressure, or, tired of the exhausting effort to resist, emigrated.

13   Cruise O'Brien, *Maria Cross*, 251.
14   O'Faolain, *Trespassers*, 102.

When O'Faolain and Cruise O'Brien wrote their then incendiary comments on Greene's Catholicism, Ireland was a complacent confessional state as that wise commentator John McGahern reminds us in an autobiographical essay: 'After independence, Church and State became inseparable, with unhealthy consequences for both. The Church grew even more powerful and authoritarian: it controlled all of education, and, through its control of the hospitals, practically all of healthcare too. The right to divorce was taken away from minorities. The special position of the Church was even inserted into the Constitution. Childishness was nurtured and encouraged to last a whole life long. Foolish pedantry took the place of thought and feeling (…) Faith and obedience were demanded, mostly taking the form of empty outward observances and a busy interest that other people do likewise, which cannot be described as other than coercive'.[15] Accordingly for an Irish artist, repudiating Catholicism was actually an assertion of artistic freedom: for an English artist, embracing Catholicism performed the same paradoxical role.

We do not know what conversation took place between Graham Greene and Conor Cruise O'Brien after Greene's Belfast visit. No recollection of their encounter is to be found in their respective letters and autobiographical works. One might surmise that so much alcohol was consumed that their memories became soggy. In his *Memoir* (1998), Cruise O'Brien mentioned *Maria Cross*, stressing the importance of this book in relation to the main themes of his own writings.[16] Strangely he fails to mention Graham Greene on whom he had written thirty-two pages in *Maria Cross*. He had also reviewed *The Honorary Consul* and *The Human Factor* in the *New York Review of Books*.[17] It is a perplexing omission.

Graham Greene inspired the same feelings of reluctant admiration in Irish writers less concerned with religion or totally estranged from it. This was notably the case with the playwright and memorialist Sean O'Casey. O'Casey had given up the Protestant faith into which he was born, and eventually converted to the revolutionary brand of socialism professed by

---

15 John Mc Gahern, *Love of the World: Essays* (London: Faber and Faber, 2009), 146.
16 Cruise O'Brien, *Memoir*, 117.
17 Conor Cruise O'Brien, 'A Funny Sort of God', *New York Review of Books*, 18 October 1973; 'Greene's Castle', *New York Review of Books*, 1 June 1976.

Jim Larkin and James Connolly. He had sympathies with the downtrodden Catholics of northside Dublin among whom he had lived. Although a non-believer he claimed to be anti-clerical but not anti-Christian. Paradoxically, this professed agnostic was a great admirer of the liturgy and basic tenets of the Catholic faith from a strictly aesthetic point of view: 'The idea of the Incarnation, the ascent, the coming of the paraclete, and all the moral philosophy, the poetic tales connected with these, are beautiful; and though not accepted either in substance or fact, remain beautiful, and I am not one to loathe the lovely.'[18]

He credited Graham Greene for having 'become Standard Enemy n°1'[19] of the Bishops, the Irish Censorship Board, and the petty bourgeoisie of Catholic Ireland. But he had reservations about his faith: 'Many believe that, like Mauriac, there is a deep tinge of Jansenism in Graham Greene'.[20] He preferred the lapsed Catholic who had turned his back against the Church to the reticent faithful who had chosen to fight the authoritarian views of Papacy and Episcopacy from the inside: 'The great writer of this age (to me) was a Catholic, James Joyce; but he broke away, and laughed at, the tradition. To keep to tradition, Mauriac and Greene have to cling to a certain style and meaning of Catholic writing; and will never stand forth as Proust did, as Joyce did, as Goethe, Tolstoy and Balzac did.'[21] What O'Casey resented most was the gloomy atmosphere of Greene's novels which he considered as irreconcilable with his own conception of Catholicism: 'Graham Greene is, of course, a powerful writer', he admitted in a letter to the Jesuit Michael E. Gallagher in June 1958, 'But I don't think he understands Catholicity: he revels in the sorrowful mysteries, but completely forgets the joyful ones, and those that give out beams of glory. So does Mauriac, a greater writer even than Greene, in my opinion.'[22] In November 1948, he wrote to Ingrid Burke: 'A few weeks ago, I read the Roman Catholic, Graham Greene's *The Heart of the Matter* which has no heart at all, but deals with a frayed

---

18   David Krause, ed., *The Letters of Sean O'Casey, 1955–1958*, Volume III (Washington, DC: Catholic University of America Press, 1989), x.
19   *The Letters of Sean O'Casey*, 139.
20   *The Letters of Sean O'Casey*, 31.
21   *The Letters of Sean O'Casey*, 153.
22   *The Letters of Sean O'Casey*, 610.

pocket of musty existences, which he evidently regards as life. The latest dogma of the R. C. Church is, apparently, Despair.'[23] O'Casey's observations are not that far removed from those of Conor Cruise O'Brien. The fact that O'Casey was born into a Protestant family gave him a particular understanding of Greene's religious sensibility. One wonders if Greene ever fully discarded his Anglican upbringing.

23　*The Letters of Sean O'Casey*, 562–3.

Irish Poets, Novelists and Peacemakers

In 1977, Greene agreed to be a member of the jury of the Ewart Biggs Memorial Prize, named after the British Ambassador who was murdered in Dublin by the IRA on 21 July 1976. The prize sought to recognise works promoting and encouraging peace and reconciliation in Ireland, greater understanding between the peoples of Britain and Ireland, and closer co-operation between partners of the European Community. Sitting with Graham Greene on the panel who judged the entries were the poet Seamus Heaney; the Irish-language poet Máire Mhac an tSaoi, wife of Conor Cruise O'Brien; Georges Sion, member of the Académie Royale de Belgique; Maurice Schumann, former French Foreign Affairs Minister, and Thomas Pakenham, well known Anglo-Irish historian.

Graham happily rubbed shoulders with Irish writers of whom he was a great admirer. He considered Yeats as the greatest poet of his time. He admired Joyce, particularly the short stories of *Dubliners*, and he held the now forgotten George Birmingham to be among the greatest humourists in the English language. He had all Birmingham's books in his library in Antibes, and he insisted that I should read *The Search Party*, 'a mini-masterpiece' in his opinion.

He loved to quote the poem by the Irish journalist, mystic, poet, economist, and artist, George William Russell, better known as A.E.:

In ancient shadows and twilights
Where childhood had strayed,
The world's great sorrows were born
And its heroes were made.
In the lost boyhood of Judas
Christ was betrayed.

Unsurprisingly, Greene was fond of the novels of the Belfast-born Brian Moore – novels permeated by themes of exile, dislocation, and the influence of Catholicism. Graham often said to me that Moore was his favourite living novelist. Initially flattered, Moore, who didn't hesitate to describe himself as 'a sort of Graham Greene running the other way',[1] came to regard the association as 'an albatross'.[2] Nevertheless, the influence of the author of *Our Man in Havana* is clearly identifiable in Moore's masterpiece *No Other Life*, published in 1993.[3] And he must have been overwhelmed with pride by the expression of admiration from the author of *The End of the Affair* in a letter to Seymour Lawrence at the *Atlantic Monthly Press*, in June 1957:

> *Judith Hearne* seemed to me to be one of the best first novels I have ever read and this (*Lupercal*) is certainly one of the best second novels – always a more difficult feat. There is a quality of realism in Mr. Moore's writing which gives the reader a kind of absolute confidence – there will be no intrusion of the author, no character will ever put a foot wrong.[4]

Graham Greene and Brian Moore later met in Montreal and became, if not exactly friends, at least affable acquaintances.[5] Greene remembered vividly an evening they spent together in Montreal at 'an amusing strip tease joint which has since been closed down'.[6]

Greene was proud of being among the first – with James Joyce and Jorge Luis Borges – to laud Flann O'Brien's first novel *At Swim Two Birds*. He wrote the blurb for a later edition of the book: 'I read it with continual excitement, amusement and the kind of glee one experiences when people smash china on the stage (…) It is a wild, fantastic, magnificently comic notion, but looking back afterwards one realises that by no other method could the realistic, the legendary, the novelette have been worked in together'.[7] Flann O'Brien (pseudonym of Brian O'Nolan) returned the favour

---

1   Patricia Craig, *Brian Moore: A Biography* (London: Bloomsbury, 2004), 139.
2   *The Irish Times*, 13 January 1999.
3   Steven Smith, 'Book of a Lifetime: No Other Life by Brian Moore', *The Independent*, 15 May 2009.
4   Craig, *Brian Moore: A Biography*, 139.
5   Craig, *Brian Moore: A Biography*, 140.
6   Craig, *Brian Moore: A Biography*, 140.
7   Maebh Long, ed., *The Collected Letters of Flann O'Brien* (Dalkey: Archives Press, 2018), 9.

by dedicating *The Hard Life* to his enthusiastic reader in a very Joycean manner: 'I honourably present to Graham Greene whose own form of gloom I admire, this misterpiece'. Graham acknowledged receipt of the book in a letter of 25 October 1961:

> Dear Mr O'Brien,
>
> I was delighted this morning to receive a copy of *The Hard Life* from your publishers and to find it dedicated to me. I am a proud man! *At Swim Two Birds* has remained to my mind ever since it first appeared one of the best books of our century. But my God what long time it has been waiting for the next.
>
> Yours
> Graham Greene.[8]

Greene also admired Sean O'Faolain for his critical thinking and his short stories. He happily recalled an expedition to Joyce's Martello Tower with O'Faolain in the 1970s.

The first Christopher Ewart-Biggs Memorial Prize was awarded to two winners, Fr Micheál MacGréil S. J. for his sociological study *Prejudice and Tolerance in Ireland*, and to Dr ATQ Stewart of Queen's University, Belfast, for *The Narrow Ground*, his acerbic and deeply pessimistic study of the Protestants in Ireland. In his acceptance speech, Mac Gréil said that his motivation had been 'to improve the general understanding of intergroup relations, leading in turn to social integration, based on respect for legitimate personal and group differences and on the principle of equality for all'.[9] In Northern Ireland, despite significant progress in the wake of the Good Friday Agreement of 1998, these aspirations are still far from being realised.

Graham had advanced the scholarly journal of which I was the co-editor as a contender for the prize: 'I proposed *Etudes Irlandaises* as one possible prize winner in the Ewart-Biggs affair', he wrote to me on 24 October 1977, 'but I am afraid the majority favour two other books which were also on my short list. I think you should enter *Etudes Irlandaises* again

---

8   Long, *The Collected Letters of Flann O'Brien*, 282.
9   *The Irish Times*, 11 November 1977.

next year'.¹⁰ In 1978, he sought to convince me to have another go: 'I hope you will be entering *Etudes Irlandaises* again for the Ewart-Biggs Prize. A lot of very unsuitable books are being sent to me at the moment'.¹¹ These efforts bore no fruit on the second occasion either.

In January 1977, in Menton, near the Franco-Italian border, I organised a seminar on Northern Ireland at the Académie de la Paix, a French think-tank founded by the Nobel Laureate René Cassin. The participants included Dr Garret FitzGerald, Minister for Foreign Affairs in Ireland; John Hume, Chairman of the Social Democratic Labour Party; and Jeremy Burchill, a spokesperson of the Unionist Party. I published a summary of these discussions in *Le Monde Diplomatique*.¹² I sent a copy to Graham who wrote to me: 'I found the Menton conference of extreme interest. Your introduction was admirable, and I didn't wish to change a word. FitzGerald and Hume were good and showed up the intransigeance of Burchill; I wish this whole debate could be printed in English as a pamphlet'.¹³

---

10   Graham Greene Letter to Pierre Joannon, 24 October 1977.
11   Graham Greene Letter to Pierre Joannon, 7 July 1978.
12   Pierre Joannon, 'Briser l'engrenage de la peur, refuser toute domination et ouvrir le dialogue', *Le Monde Diplomatique*, May 1977.
13   Graham Greene, Letter to Pierre Joannon, 2 June 1977.

Antibes, the Town He Loved So Well

In another interview, published in 1988 in a now defunct French magazine called *Speak-Up*, I asked Graham what made him choose Antibes and the South of France as his permanent residence: 'Well, that goes into private life. I first came to Antibes shortly after the war, around 1946, and liked it very much. I used to come down to sail with Alexander Korda, the film producer, a great friend of mine. He kept a boat in the harbour. I remember walking up the ramparts of Antibes. There was a nice house for sale and I was rather tempted because I could have bought it at that time for the equivalent of three thousand pounds. Unfortunately I didn't. In 1959, some great friends of mine whom I had met in Africa came to live in Antibes.[1] Then, in 1961, I had a very bad attack of pneumonia which I caught in Russia and the doctor said that I ought to leave England during the winters, so I started to rent an apartment near the ramparts for two months at a time. Eventually I got more and more tired of coming and going back and decided to reside permanently in Antibes. I made a point of coming by train, not by air, to mark the decision. And on 1 January 1966, I settled here and bought a flat'.[2]

Another reason to settle in the South of France was that he had been advised to become domiciled in another country to avoid the consequences of a tax evasion scheme organised by his dodgy accountant, Thomas Roe, who embezzled his clients' money, including Graham's, and had been arrested in 1965 and sent to prison.[3]

---

1 Greene had met Yvonne and Jacques Cloetta in Douala in Cameroon. Cloetta, *In Search of a Beginning. My Life with Graham Greene.*
2 'Graham Greene, Britain's top novelist breaks the silence', an exclusive interview with Pierre Joannon, *Speak-Up*, n°12, Mars 1988, 30–7.
3 Norman Sherry, *The Life of Graham Greene*, Vol. III, 1955–1991 (London: Viking Penguin, 2004), 408–16.

Finding in Antibes a new source of inspiration, he wrote a collection of short stories which were published in 1967 under the title *May We Borrow Your Husband and Other Comedies of the Sexual Life*. He described these light and humorous interludes as a form of escape from the novelist's gloomy world. The Jansenist pilloried by Catholic and non-Catholic Irish censors was transformed into a Libertine amused by the very mixed humanity of his new city of adoption. '*May We Borrow Your Husband?*' wrote Graham in a new introduction, 'was indeed written in a single mood of sad hilarity, while I was establishing a home in a two-roomed apartment over the port at Antibes. Taking my dinner nightly, in the little restaurant of Félix au Port, some of the tales emerged from conversations at other tables (even from a phrase misunderstood), though the title story had been in my mind for a number of years. I had brought the idea with me to Antibes as part of my baggage, and I set the scene in Antibes, though in fact I had seen the incident happen under my eyes (or so I imagined) at St Jean-Cap Ferrat while I worked at a hotel window on a very different subject, *A Burnt-Out Case*'.[4]

However, the stories which make up the collection were inspired by more than a simple desire to entertain and relax under the sun of the Riviera. These stories, 'all written during what should be the last decade of my life, are an escape in humour from the thought of death – this time of certain death. Writing is a form of therapy; sometimes I wonder how all those who do not write, compose or paint can manage to escape the madness, the melancholia, the panic fear which is inherent in the human situation'.[5]

Even if he had more than two decades left to live, and not just one, this feeling of approaching the end of one's life was a conviction deeply rooted in his mind. This is the Graham Greene we knew, a man inhabited by the proximity of death and the finitude of all things.

The hotel facing the sea where the intrigue of *May We Borrow Your Husband?* is taking place is not named by the author of the short story. But it is rather obvious that it is the Hôtel Royal situated on the Boulevard Maréchal Leclerc which was destroyed some years ago and replaced by a

4   Graham Greene, *Collected Stories* (London: The Bodley Head & William Heinemann, 1974), x.
5   Greene, *Collected Stories*, xii.

new hotel bearing the same name. The protagonists are a British middle-aged writer busy working on a biography of Lord Rochester (like Graham himself), two English interior-decorator homosexuals in quest of adventure and a young newly married couple on their honeymoon.

The setting, particularly evocative, is Antibes after the end of the summer season: 'It was the time of year I like best', says the narrator, 'when Juan les Pins becomes as squalid as a closed fun-fair with Luna Park boarded up and cards marked *Fermeture Annuelle* outside the Pam-Pam and Maxim's, and the Concours International Amateur de Striptease at the Vieux Colombier is over for another season. Then Antibes comes into its own as a small country town with the Auberge de Provence full of local people and old men sit indoors drinking beer or pastis at the *glacier* in the Place de Gaulle. The small garden, which forms a roundabout on the ramparts looks a little sad with the short stout palms bowing their brown fronds; the sun in the morning shines without any glare, and the few white sails move gently on the unblinding sea.'[6]

The writer is the sad witness of the sophisticated enterprise of seduction launched by the two interior-decorators who have been quick to identify a latent homosexual in the newly wed husband: 'It was like a medieval siege: they dug their trenches and threw up their earthworks.'[7] He tries to open the eyes of the poor wife, but she is too naïve to notice that her husband is drifting away from her. To avoid being complicit in this inevitable debacle, the writer goes to his room, packs his belongings, leaves the Hotel Royal and takes refuge in one of the last hotels still open in Juan les Pins.

This short story is a gem, one of the best, if not the best, of the collection. I often said to Graham how much I loved this somewhat perverse and farcical plot which was for me like the faded photograph of a bygone Antibes with its sounds of children at play, fishermen enjoying a game of *pétanque*, English tourists battling against the cold northerly Mistral; and the sight of the twinning ramparts, the little rocky peninsula opposite the Hotel Royal and the small narrow backstreets of the old town where the washing is hung out of the windows as in Naples.

---

6   Greene, *Collected Stories*, 4.
7   Greene, *Collected Stories*, 14.

In Antibes, did he miss England sometimes? To that question, Graham admitted: 'I miss the English countryside which I have always liked. I am very fond of Suffolk and Bury St Edmunds where there is a family brewery, but not London, funnily enough. I was attached to London at the time of the war, during the Blitz, because there was a great spirit of comradeship. The only things which I miss really are English draught beer and English sausages'.[8]

Every time my wife Annick and I visited London, we would go to Paxton and Whitfield at 93 Jermyn Street and buy a dozen sausages to bring back to our forlorn friend in the Résidence des Fleurs.

I was keen to know if he shared the view expressed by Cyril Connolly shortly after the end of the second World War: 'France must remain a place where everyone can go, and where everyone can, if he wishes, live, and live without guilt and without a feeling of expatriation. The great blessing France confers on the artist is anonymity. When an English writer goes there, one by one the layers of his social personality peel off, he finds there are more and more things he can do without, and more and more he comes to be preoccupied with his central situation, his creative possibilities. For in France he is not an ordinary nobody. This nobody, who leaves behind his old social or academic skin, is offered all that is most rare and delightful in life: masterpieces of paintings and architecture, natural beauty, congenial climate, cheap food, good wine, a room to write in, a café to talk in, and a well-wishing atmosphere in which everything is simplified'.[9]

Greene allowed himself a ghost of a smile on hearing this statement: 'Arthur Koestler poked fun at Cyril Connolly's ecstatic francophilia. He was a bit harsh but I don't blame him. I agree with what Cyril said about the advantage of anonymity and the absurdity of the feeling of expatriation. The rest is pure humbug. As far as I am concerned, what I have sought in Antibes and Anacapri is to be away, far from the people, the obligations, the boring assignments, and duties interfering with my writing.'

---

8 *Graham Greene breaks the silence*, interview by Pierre Joannon, Speak-Up, n°12, March 1988, pp. 30–7.
9 Cyril Connolly, *The Condemned Playground: Essays 1927–1944* (London: The Hogarth Press, 1985), 87–8.

Meeting the Irish

Normally shy and reluctant to meet strangers, Graham proved surprisingly happy to accept my invitations to meet French and Irish friends eager to meet him.

On 26 September 1980, at the Hotel Helios in Juan-les-Pins I launched an Irish club bearing the name of my favourite brand of Irish whiskey. *The Irish Times* sent Fergus Pyle, one of its best journalists, to cover the event. In his enthusiastic article, he extolled the virtues of the founding father of this new venture: 'Pierre Joannon, the Irish Consul General in Antibes. And when you say Joannon you conjure up a kind of cultural transvestite, a single-minded publicist for Ireland and populariser of Irish history among the French who are not notorious for their interest in other countries. Joannon is a phenomenon. He wrote a biography of Michael Collins a couple of years ago and he co-edits an annual review of Irish studies published by the University of Lille but he also knows everyone and everyone knows him, which is why he was the lynchpin of the party thrown by Irish Distillers last Friday night to launch the Jameson Irish Club.'[1]

The guests included Graham Greene, 'rock-like and impassive', to whom John Ryan, General Manager of the international division of Irish Distillers, presented a bottle of 12-year-old Jameson; Michel Déon, Ireland's first resident French academician, author of *A Purple Taxi*; the Irish artists Louis Le Brocquy and his wife Ann Madden who were living at the time in Carros near Nice; the writer Paul Guimard and his feminist wife Benoite Groult, frequently to be found fishing in Derrynane, Co. Kerry; author Jean Raspail, biographer of the King of Patagonia and descendant of the socialist who gave his name to a major boulevard in Paris.

Garret FitzGerald and his wife Joan were also there, en route to the Middle East; so was Denis Corboy, the European Commission's man in Dublin and future ambassador of the EU in Washington; and Sheamus

---

1 Fergus Pyle, 'Niven-Greene Join the Converts', *The Irish Times*, 30 September 1980.

Smith, managing director of the National Film Studios of Ardmore and future Film Censor of Ireland. Among those who agreed to be founding members of the Club were the writer Anthony Burgess who had an Irish grandmother, British artist David Niven and Lord Glenavy (better known as Paddy Campbell).

Launch of the Jameson Irish Club at the Hotel Helios in Juan les Pins, 26 September 1980. From left to right: Irish painter Louis Le Brocquy; Jacqueline Murphy; Graham Greene; Irish Film Censor Sheamus Smith; future Taoiseach Garret FitzGerald; Pierre Joannon; French writer Paul Guimard; Annick Joannon; French writer Michel Déon of the Académie française; French writer Benoite Groult.

Graham Greene enjoyed a lively conversation with Michel Déon of the Académie Française. They both started out as journalists and were later publishers, Graham with Eyre and Spottiswoode and The Bodley Head, Michel Déon with Plon and La Table Ronde. They were both expatriates, Graham in France, Michel in the Greek Island of Spetsai and later in Tynagh, Co. Galway. They were amused to discover that they had both visited Padre Pio in his retreat of San Giovanni Rotondo. Déon later wrote a superb review of the French translation of *The Human Factor*, and Graham expressed his admiration for the English translation of Déon's novel *Un Déjeuner de Soleil*, published in Britain under the title *Where Are You Dying Tonight?*

John Ryan offering a bottle of Jameson Irish Whiskey to Graham Greene in the presence of Yvonne Cloetta (Juan les Pins, 26 September 1980).

Graham attended several gatherings of my Jameson Irish Club which sought to foster closer relations between France and Ireland on every level – cultural, artistic, and economic. He enjoyed these lively parties, belying his reputation as a withdrawn curmudgeon insulated from public and social life.

Michel Déon of the Académie française, Pierre Joannon and Graham Greene, September 1980.

I also introduced him to Michel Mohrt, another *'Immortel'* of the Académie Française, a fine writer and the *'éminence grise'* of translations from English at Gallimard, the prestigious French publishing house.[2]

These private gatherings were sometimes fascinating, sometimes disastrous. We spent an evening with our close friend Professor René-Jean Dupuy, one of the greatest specialists of international law in France, former rector of the International Law Academy of The Hague, member of the Collège de France and of the Académie des Sciences Morales et Politiques. Dupuy, a devout Catholic, was a huge admirer of *The Power and the Glory*. Graham was in sombre mood and the conversation soon derailed. It started with an over-enthusiastic reference by our friend to the strange world known as 'Greeneland'. Graham reacted as if he had been bitten by a rattlesnake: 'Once one has seen a dead child in a ditch in Vietnam

2   Pierre Joannon, *Michel Mohrt, réfractaire stendhalien* (Paris: Éditions La Thébaïde, 2021).

or Mexico in the time of religious persecutions or been confronted with the atrocities in Haiti under Papa Doc or Cuba under Batista, one is no longer inventing fictions called *The Quiet American* or *The Power and the Glory* or *The Comedians* or *Our Man in Havana*. There is no such place as Greeneland. It is only the world as it is.'

The next question posed to him concerned his description as 'a Catholic writer', to which Graham replied curtly: 'I don't know what a Catholic writer is. As far as I am concerned, I am a writer who happens to be a Catholic, that's all.' To alleviate the discomfort, I said jokingly: 'Graham, you remind me of Brendan Behan who once said "I am not a writer with a drink problem, I am a drinker with a writing problem".' It was insufficient to salvage the evening.

Graham was far from being the only religiously minded novelist to show uneasiness at being labelled a 'Catholic writer'. François Mauriac in 1923, confessed: 'I am a novelist as well as a Catholic, and this is the source of the conflict. I think it is fortunate for a novelist to be Catholic, but I am convinced that it is also very dangerous for a Catholic to be a novelist.' Shortly afterwards, Mauriac announced a big turning point in his work: 'In my next novels, Catholicism will barely influence my characters, but it will still be a Catholic approach to show the absence of the Catholic faith and the deplorable consequences it is leading to; just by staging characters completely devoid of religious life, one discovers the great emptiness of the souls, emptiness particularly noticeable in women.'[3] Answering a remark made by Jacques Maritain about his mysticism, Julien Green clarified his position: 'I do not attempt to turn my books into Catholic novels. It would horrify me. But I think that all my novels, as far as they may seem from plain religiosity, are nevertheless religious by essence. The anxiety and solitude of my characters nearly always come down to what I think I have called the fear and horror to be part of the world in all its aspects.'[4]

When the conversation avoided sensitive matters, Graham could be a perfect guest, talkative and cheerful. He enjoyed the Irish 'gift of the

---

3 J. L. Barré, *François Mauriac: Biographie intime 1885–1940* (Paris: Fayard, 2009), 344. (My translation).

4 Julien Green, *Œuvres Complètes*, Vol. IV (Paris: Gallimard, 1975), 1114. (My translation).

gab'. At a dinner party at the Villa Dinah, in the Parc Saramartel above Juan-les-Pins, he particularly enjoyed the company of Patrick Campbell, 3rd Baron Glenavy, regular contributor to the *Irish Times* and the *Sunday Times*, team leader on the BBC television programme *Call my Bluff*, and writer of hilarious books. He was among the most extraordinary wits out of Ireland, a country which has produced so many throughout the centuries.

Frank Muir has penned a portrait of this exceptional Dublin character: 'Patrick Campbell. Unbelievably tall. A few choice hairs the colour of a Kellogg's Corn Flake. Eyes as close together as a pair of cufflinks. A slight tendency to drift sideways when walking, like a young, lost crab. When surprised would rear up, eyes rounded, the picture of an ostrich which has sat in something. His stories told of the tiny agonies and embarrassments of his life, so huge at the time, and he told them plainly, sometimes rather sadly, with a rare grace of style.

Lady Glenavy; Irish Film Censor Sheamus Smith; Lord Glenavy known as Paddy Campbell; Sheila Hampson; Annick Joannon; Graham Greene (Villa Dinah, Juan les Pins, 25 April 1980).

He was, I think, the humourist's humourist'.[5]

Paddy Campbell told us in his inimitable way that in the early 60s, when entering a grocery shop in the little village of Le Rouret where he and his wife were living, he was welcomed by the *patronne* by a resounding *Bonjour M'sieur Charles*. Why she had addressed him in this manner was a mystery that he tried to elucidate by questioning the good lady? Ill at ease, the latter answered that she had called him *M'sieur Charles* because he so closely resembled General de Gaulle both in height and – she blushed with a measure of embarrassment – in the length of his nose. 'Since that day', said Paddy Campbell, 'I became a staunch Gaullist, not because I knew or approved the policies implemented by "le plus illustre des Français" but because if de Gaulle was to be rejected at the polls, I would lose my identity and go back to being a mere *M'sieur* again.' 'It would turn me into a ghost', he told us, adding: 'The truth of the matter is that in France or, rather, in that little village of the Alpes-Maritimes, General de Gaulle and I were condemned to sink or swim together.' This fatal event eventually took place in 1969: having lost the referendum on the regions, de Gaulle immediately resigned as President of France and decided to travel to Ireland, the country of his maternal ancestors, to be away from France during the forthcoming presidential election and the anniversary of his 18 June 1940 call from London. Funnily enough, Paddy Campbell was asked to lay siege the hotel where de Gaulle was staying near Sneem, in county Kerry, to try to interview him. He failed miserably as the General was well protected against the paparazzi and the journalists. Paddy spent hours waiting in vain at the gate of the Hotel when he suddenly spotted a small black car with a strong police escort. He was able to recognise the General and Tante Yvonne in the back seat before the gates of their retreat flew open. Paddy bent down and caught the eye of the General: 'Vive la France', he shouted, getting carried away with himself. He described the scene with his incredible sense of humour: 'The great monolithic face eased a fraction. There was almost the suggestion of a smile. De Gaulle raised the two hands in their famous all-encompassing gesture, and then he and

---

5   *The Campbell Companion: The Best of Patrick Campbell*, edited and introduced by Ulick O'Connor (London: Pavilion Books, 1987).

Tante Yvonne were swept away. Under the circumstances, it seemed to me to be an outstanding interview.'

We all had a good laugh. As a matter of fact, Graham so much enjoyed this cultured wit who stuttered the funniest stories about the strangeness and vagaries of human nature that the evening lasted until well past four o'clock in the morning.

Graham Greene; Pierre Joannon; Lady Glenavy (Villa Dinah, Parc Saramarte, Juan les Pins, 25 April 1980).

Graham also enjoyed meeting Garret FitzGerald who was to serve as Taoiseach from July 1981 to February 1982 and from December 1982 to March 1987. Garret was a vibrant intellectual who exerted a profound influence on his country and eventually managed to persuade the recalcitrant Margaret Thatcher into reluctantly signing the Anglo-Irish Agreement of 1985, regarded as the first step of the Northern Ireland Peace Process. Graham told me on many occasions that he was very impressed by the moral stature and political acumen of FitzGerald.

Garret had first appointed me Honorary Consul of Ireland in September 1973 while he was Minister for Foreign Affairs. I don't think he ever regretted having conferred upon me the responsibility to represent Ireland in the South of France, making me in due course the longest serving honorary consul of the Irish diplomatic service. Contributing to my Festschrift in 2009, he wrote: 'I have known Pierre and Annick ever since I was appointed minister for Foreign Affairs in March 1973. At that time, I was approached by several members of the outgoing administration to say that they had intended to appoint him as Honorary Consul in Antibes and they recommended that I implement this proposal. The Department were well disposed and I was happy to appoint Pierre. I soon learned how strongly committed he was to the Irish-French relationship and how enthusiastically and effectively he contributed to this by writing extensively about Ireland including his remarkable *Histoire de l'Irlande et des Irlandais*. No one has done more for the Irish-French relationship in the past four decades than Pierre'.[6]

It is no secret that Graham Greene was a great film buff. Most of his novels were adapted for the screen, not always to his satisfaction. But what is less well known is the fact that for five years in the 1930s he had chronicled every week the films that opened in London for *The Spectator* and briefly for the distinguished, ill-fated magazine *Night and Day*. He relished the cinema in all its forms, but his critiques were sharp, highly opinionated, biased even. He made no bones about his likes and dislikes. On the films of Irish interest, he could be laudatory or scathing. On *The Informer* by John Ford, he was quite complimentary in his assessment of *The Spectator* of 11 October 1935: 'Mr Liam O'Flaherty's novel of the Irish Rebellion has been filmed a second time. It is superb material for the screen; very few words are needed for this drama; terror is not a subtle sensation; it can be conveyed very much easier by images alone than scruples, guilt, tenderness. You only need the Black and Tans patrols through the Liffey fogs, the watching secretive figures outside the saloons as the drunken informer drift deeper and deeper with his cronies into the seedy night life of Dublin.

---

6 Jane Conroy, ed., *Franco-Irish Connections: Essays, Memoirs and Poems in Honour of Pierre Joannon* (Dublin: Four Courts Press, 2009), 82.

Mr Victor Mc Laglen has never given an abler performance, and the film, even if it sometimes underlines its points rather crudely, is a memorable picture of a pitiless war waged without honour on either side in doorways and cellars and gin-shops'.[7]

On the contrary, he finds *Man of Aran* by Robert Flaherty 'bogus and sentimental' and 'hopelessly literary'.[8] He is also particularly severe on Brian Desmond Hurst's *Ourselves Alone*, 'one of the silliest pictures which even an English studio has yet managed to turn out. This latter picture has been extravagantly praised, even compared favourably with *The Informer*, and yet I defy any normal person (among whom one has long ceased to number the boisterous good fellows of the London Press) to find more than one effective sequence, more than one good sentence, in this sentimental and melodramatic story of the Irish Rebellion. The dialogue and the script are not the fault of Mr Desmond Hurst, who has indeed directed one good scene, when the Black and Tans search a public house and the Irish women hide the Sinn Fein revolvers under their skirts and a sentimental ballad-singer sings plaintively on, while the camera makes a complete circle of the room, from the singer's face back to the singer's face, picking out the right authentic details on its way. This scene has unmistakable quality and promise; otherwise *Ourselves Alone*, following Mr Desmond Hurst's previous picture, *Riders to the Sea*, might make one despair of this director'[9]. The fate of this film is rather amusing: it was banned in Northern Ireland where it was considered Sinn Fein propaganda. In the Free State, the film was vilified in the nationalist press as pro-British.[10]

Because I knew that Greene was a film connoisseur and practitioner, I always invited the scriptwriter of *The Third Man* to the parties that I organised during the Cannes Film Festival whenever there was an Irish film in the official competition. Around the swimming pool of 'Les Chênes Verts', Graham recalled his foray into the movies with professionals like

---

7   Graham Greene, *The Pleasure Dome: The Collected Film Criticism 1935–1940*, edited by John Russell Taylor (London: Secker and Warburg, 1972), 26.
8   Greene, *The Pleasure Dome*, 29–30.
9   Greene, *The Pleasure Dome*, 90–1.
10 Donal Fallon, 'Film as Art: Brian Desmond Hurst', *History Ireland*, 31, no. 5 (September–October 2023), 57.

Sheamus Smith, managing director of the National Film Studios of Ireland, and John Boorman, the British film director who resided, until recently, in County Wicklow, and is regarded as one of the founding figures of modern Irish cinema.[11]

John Boorman; Pierre Joannon and Graham Greene at the Villa Les Chênes Verts in the Cap d'Antibes, for the launching of John Boorman's film *Excalibur* at the International Cannes Film festival, 24 May 1981.

In 1981, at a party held in the Pavilion Eden Roc in the Cap d'Antibes, I conceived the quixotic project to reconcile Graham Greene and Anthony Burgess, both good friends of mine, who frequently ventilated their intense dislike for each other. The photograph of the two expatriate British writers shows me haplessly in the middle looking like an anxious fire fighter caught between a lit torch and a stick of dynamite. It all went well enough, they were polite and courteous to each other, but so guarded that any whiff of

11 Sheamus Smith, *Off Screen: A Memoir* (Dublin: Gill and Macmillan, 2007), 187 and 196–7.

reconciliation remained elusive. Graham was the epitome of the reserved Englishman, introverted, shy and self-restrained. Anthony was extroverted, flamboyant, proud of his Irish ancestry, always restless and talking at machine gun speed. One was an island, the other a volcano. One worshipped Henry James, the other James Joyce. Graham pretended that he could not read Burgess without a dictionary. Of the author of *A Clockwork Orange*, Graham quoted Disraeli on Gladstone – that he was 'inebriated by the exuberance of his own verbosity'. Last but not least, the two men were divided by the same faith. Burgess, born Catholic, accused Graham, the convert, of theological arrogance. For Burgess, Greene was a closet Jansenist. My well-intentioned effort fell on remarkably stony ground.

Graham Greene, Pierre Joannon and Anthony Burgess at Eden Roc,
Cap d'Antibes, 18 May 1982.

The Final Challenge

In the 1980s, Graham was disturbed, obsessed, and enraged by the messy separation between Martine, the daughter of Yvonne Cloetta, the last great passion of his life, and a local businessman with a criminal record and shady connections. Eventually a legally questionable divorce by mutual consent was obtained but under conditions of exceptional duress. Martine had to live within a radius of five hundred meters of her ex-husband's home; she was forbidden to work after 8 p.m.; she could not take her children to visit their grandparents in Juan-les-Pins. Furthermore, her ex-husband started to make life intolerable for her and for her parents. He brutalised his former wife, spirited away their 6-year-old daughter, threatened to blow Yvonne's brains out, and assaulted Jacques Cloetta, Martine's father. All these incidents were unavailingly reported to the local police. The young woman, her parents and Graham were engulfed in a sordid climate of blackmail, intimidation and violence that was exacerbated daily. Martine's husband even managed to secure temporary custody of the couple's daughter.

The situation was so blatantly biased that Graham contemplated publishing an article or a book on police complacency and dysfunctional courts on the Riviera. I introduced him to my friend Pierre Merli, Mayor of Antibes and member of the French parliament, who promised to help. I wrote to the Préfet, head of the services of the State in the *département*, who duly forwarded my letter to Paris. A meeting followed between Graham and the Minister of Justice, Alain Peyrefitte, and this initiated an internal enquiry into the functioning of the judiciary in Nice. While some superficial remedial measures were implemented, they did not materially mitigate the horrific state of Martine's affairs.

Martine's ex-husband was very proud of his military service in Algeria during the war of independence. He boasted that he had been an active member of the Organisation Armée Secrète (OAS), the clandestine organization founded by dissident officers of the French army after the failure of the putsch of April 1961 to prevent Algerian independence by a desperate rear-guard campaign of violence.[1] The head of the OAS was none other than general Raoul Salan, Greene's old friend with whom he enjoyed smoking opium in the *fumeries* of Cholon during the war in Indo-China. Arrested in Algiers, Salan was condemned by the Haut Tribunal Militaire, a special ad hoc jurisdiction, to life imprisonment, a sentence considered too lenient by President Charles de Gaulle who wanted him shot by a firing squad. The reluctant Haut Tribunal Militaire was, in consequence, dissolved on the 27th of May 1962.

Held in detention at the prison of Tulle, Raoul Salan eventually benefitted from a pardon on 15 June 1968, and from a later amnesty voted by the French parliament in 1982. Remembering his past connections with 'the Mandarin' as general Salan was nicknamed, Graham sent him on 24 March 1980 a handwritten letter in French – a rather unusual step – which reads as follow in English.

> My dear Général,
>
> I hesitate to bother you with a personal problem but I am encouraged to do so by all the memories I retain of your kindness towards me in Vietnam.
>
> This is the problem. The daughter of a great friend of mine is suffering from persecution and threats by her ex-husband, a certain Daniel Guy who pretends that he went to prison when he was young for having been a member of the OAS.
>
> I have good reasons to think that his claim is only the cover of an infinitely less honourable affair.
>
> Would it be possible to check if what he says is true or false?
>
> This Daniel Guy is a real estate developer who lives in Nice where he is running an agency by the name of CEGI. He is born on the 29th of December 1940 at Belleville-sur-Saône, and I know that he has been in jail on four occasions for various offences.
>
> I am now settled in France but I am still in contact with our common friend Trevor Wilson who is, I regret to say, in poor health.
>
> I hope that we may all meet again before the fall of the curtain.

---

1   Annex 5 of *J'Accuse: The Dark side of Nice*, by Graham Greene (London: The Bodley Head, 1982), 34.

Please receive, my dear General, the expression of my most cordial feelings.

Graham Greene.[2]

I have not been able to locate Salan's answer but it is obvious that it confirmed Graham's doubts. In a typed letter in French of 8 April 1980, he thanks him in these terms:

---

2   Handwritten letter to General Raoul Salan sent from the Résidence des Fleurs in Antibes on the 24th of March 1980: « Mon cher Général, J'hésite à venir vous importuner avec un problème personnel mais suis encouragé par tous les souvenirs que je garde de votre gentillesse à mon égard au Vietnam. Voici ce problème. La fille d'une grande amie à moi souffre de la persécution et des menaces de son ex-mari, un certain Daniel Guy qui prétend avoir fait de la prison lorsqu'il était jeune parce qu'il était membre de l'OAS J'ai de bonnes raisons de croire que cette prétention n'est que la couverture d'une affaire infiniment moins honorable. Serait-il possible de découvrir si ce qu'il prétend est vrai ou faux ? Le Guy en question est un promoteur immobilier qui vit actuellement à Nice où il a monté une agence CEGI. Il est né le 29 décembre 1940 à Belleville sur Saône, et je sais qu'il a été quatre fois en prison entre 1960 et 1970 pour des délits divers. Je suis maintenant installé en France mais je reste en contact avec notre ami commun Trevor Wilson dont, hélas, la santé est déficiente. Je souhaite que nous puissions tous nous rencontrer encore avant que le rideau tombe. Recevez, mon cher Général, l'expression de mes sentiments les plus cordiaux. Graham Greene ».(From the Archives of General Salan, reproduced by kind permission of the Association des Amis de Raoul Salan and its chairman Bernard Zeller).

CHAPTER 9

```
                    La Résidence des Fleurs,
                    Avenue Pasteur,
                    06 Antibes.    le 8 Avril 1980

Mon Cher Général,

             Merci infiniment pour le soin que
vous avez mis à essayer de trouver trace du
dénommé Daniel GUY.    Ainsi que je le pensais,
il n'a jamais appartenu à l'O.A.S. et je suis
outré qu'il fasse marcher son Agence immobilière
de Nice: la CEGI en se vantant de ses exploits;
il montre à qui veut les voir, un tatouage sur
le bras droit, un diplôme et une médaille
qu'il prétend avoir obtenus pour ses services
dans l'O.A.S.   A tout le monde : Banquiers,
collaborateurs , clients, il s'en sert pour
couvrir son passé sordide et comme raison pour
laquelle il est privé de ses droits civiques.

             Je souhaiterais vraiment, mon Général,
si cela était possible, en quelleque façon, qu'il
lui soit interdit de continuer à déshonorer ainsi
le nom de l'O.A.S.

             Excusez moi  si je vous importûne,
mais il y a, dans la vie des choses que je trouve
révoltantes et celle-ci en est une.

             Bien amicalement Vôtre,

                     [signature]
                     Graham Greene
```

Letter of Graham Greene to General Raoul Salan, 8 April 1980.

My dear General,

Thank you so much for the care you took in trying to find a trace of the said Daniel Guy. As I thought, he never belonged to the OAS and I am shocked that he is operating his real estate agency in Nice – the CEGI – bragging about his exploits and showing anyone who wants to see them a tattoo on his right arm, a diploma and a medal which he pretends to have obtained for his services in the OAS. To everybody – bankers, colleagues, employees and clients – he uses it to cover his sordid past and as an explanation of the fact that he has been deprived of his civil rights.

I would really wish, General, if that was possible, in any way, that he be prohibited from dishonouring as he does, the name of the OAS.

Please forgive me for bothering you, but there are, in life, things that I find revolting and this is one.

Very amicably yours,
Graham Greene'.[3]

In May 1981, François Mitterand was elected President and, following the subsequent victory of the Socialists at the general election, a left-wing government was formed in Paris. My friend, the writer Paul Guimard, had been appointed adviser to the President with an office at the Elysée. I contacted him and made another plea for help. Graham was received by the new socialist Minister for Justice, Robert Badinter, who promised to act swiftly. But the situation once again remained unchanged. No one could curb the brutal arrogance of Martine's ex-husband and the violence of his campaign of attrition.

Graham finally decided to revert to his initial plan of making the whole story public in the international press.

On 31 January 1982, *The Sunday Times* published a full page on 'Graham Greene's private war in the South of France'. Shortly afterwards, a sixty-nine-page-long bilingual pamphlet entitled *J'Accuse. The Dark Side of Nice* appeared, published by Bodley Head under Graham's signature. The first two sentences were a bombshell: 'Let me issue a warning to anyone who is tempted to settle for a peaceful life on what is called the Côte d'Azur. Avoid the region of Nice which is the preserve of some of the most criminal organisations in the South of France.' All

---

3   Typed letter to General Salan from the Résidence des Fleurs in Antibes dated 8 April 1980 (Archives of General Salan, reproduced by kind permission of the Association des Amis de Raoul Salan and its chairman Bernard Zeller).

the sordid details of the case were disclosed and the conclusion of the pamphlet was uncompromising:

> I accuse certain police officers in Nice of protecting criminals, of encouraging them in their crimes by guaranteeing them immunity whether for the sake of the information they provide or for money and favours. I accuse certain magistrates of having deliberately shut their eyes to a problem concerning the emotional stability of two children.[4]

Graham's accusations made world headlines. Hundreds of journalists swarmed the capital of the French Riviera. The author of *J'accuse* gave countless interviews. He was vilified in some papers, eulogised in others. The media battle raged. At first, it seemed that Graham had gone too far. His pamphlet was declared defamatory and banned by a French tribunal, and another court forced him, his publisher and some newspapers to pay libel damages. In the end, the weapon proved effective. Martine was granted custody of her children; she went to live in Switzerland and the troublemaker was subdued. In a letter to his publisher Max Reinhardt, Graham said of his pamphlet: 'I feel it has served its purpose and we have won most of our case'.[5]

---

4   Greene, *J'Accuse*, 29.
5   Letter to Max Reinhardt, 22 December 1986, quoted by Sherry, *The Life of Graham Greene, Vol. III, 1955–1991*, 655.

The Final Challenge

Pierre Joannon, Graham Greene, Martine and Yvonne Cloetta at Les Chênes Verts, Cap d'Antibes, 24 May 1981.

My involvement in this affair was acknowledged by both sides. I received an anonymous phone call conveying an obvious threat: 'Mind your own business and stop giving stupid advice to Mr Greene.' Graham gave me a limited edition of his book *How Father Quixote Became a Monsignor* with this inscription on the first page: 'For Pierre and Annick in the hope that one day I can do a little for you compared with what you have done for us.' I was – and am – intensely moved by this expression of gratitude even though I knew that my efforts had been largely ineffectual. In the end, victory belonged to what Father Leopoldo Duran called 'the incalculable power of one man's pen'.[6]

---

6   Duran, *Graham Greene Friend and Brother*, 259.

A Literary Feud

I was also involved in another controversy that took place towards the end of Graham's life. In 1988, I had received a phone call from my friend Sean Donlon, former Irish Ambassador to the United States and Secretary General of the Irish Department of Foreign Affairs before joining the Shannon based company Guinness Peat Aviation (GPA), as Executive Vice-President. This innovative company, set up by Dr Tony Ryan, was then the world's largest commercial aircraft sales and leasing company. Ryan, who also co-founded the low-cost airline company Ryanair, was a philanthropist with an active interest in university education, culture and the fine arts. His company had launched a GPA Book Award with a prize money of 50,000 IR£ making it among the world's richest literary prize.

Sean Donlon requested me to help him recruit 'the best-known living writer in the English language to be the adjudicator'. Graham Greene 'would give the award an immediate importance and distinction in the world of letters'.[1] Knowing that Graham was a close friend of mine, Donlon asked me to see if he would accept to be the inaugural adjudicator of the GPA Book Award.

I was slightly doubtful of my ability to persuade Graham, but I was happily surprised to see him agreeable, on condition that he could award it to Vincent McDonnell, the young Irish author of a novel entitled *The Broken Commandment* which he had read in manuscript and which had moved him so much that he had convinced his friend Max Reinhardt to publish it. Sean Donlon accepted this condition without discussion and soon flew down to Nice to finalise the agreement.

In my house in the Cap d'Antibes, it was agreed that two lists of books would be established: a long list in which the name of Vincent

---

1   Sean Donlon, 'Graham Greene and the GPA Book Award', in *Franco-Irish Connections: Essays, Memoirs, and Poems in Honour of Pierre Joannon*, 79.

McDonnell would appear, and a short list selected by a panel of literary assessors. Graham would be free to choose the laureate of the GPA Book Award out of one or the other list. Sean Donlon took great care to confirm in writing what had been agreed between us. It was later said that these terms were 'unusual' or difficult to 'fully comprehend' – a laughable proposition if one remembers the skilful diplomat that Sean Donlon was.

In a letter to Graham Greene of 9 March 1989, a copy of which was posted to me, matters were clearly summarised:

> Dear Mr Greene,
>
> You will recall the very pleasant occasion at Dr Joannon's house in December when we discussed the proposed GPA Book Award.
>
> On the basis of our discussion, we have now advanced the proposal as follows:
>
> 1. In the late Autumn of this year, an award of £50,000 will be made to an Irish born or a resident author in respect of a book published during the period 1 October 1986 to 30 September 1989;
> 2. A maximum of five books will be sent to you in October 1989. You will select the winning author either from those five books or from a full list of the books submitted for the Award.
> 3. Our preference is for one winner but should you decide to divide the £50,000 between two authors, that would be acceptable;
> 4. Because Irish authors are published in the US and Britain as well as in Ireland, we believe we need assessors in those countries as well as in Ireland to help draw up the short list of five books. Professor Hugh Kenner of John Hopkins University and in Britain the novelist Faye Weldon and critic Philip French have agreed to assist. Mr Gerry Dukes, an Irish academic and theatre critic has agreed to do most of the work and become the Award Administrator.
>
> I very much hope that you will find the above arrangement acceptable and, if you agree, we should now proceed to publicise the Award and get to work as soon as possible.
>
> With warm personal regards,
>
> Yours sincerely,
> Sean Donlon[2]

---

2   Sean Donlon to Graham Greene, March 9, 1989, Ref. SD/aw2778.

This letter, sent to Graham Greene and me nine months before the GPA Book Award ceremony, made plain that three elements had been clearly stated from the beginning: the existence of two lists of books, a perfect understanding that the Adjudicator would be free to select the laureate from either of the two lists, and the possibility of splitting the prize between two authors if the Adjudicator chose to do so.

Satisfied with the arrangements, Graham met with Gerry Dukes who visited him in Antibes on three occasions and received in due course the five books selected by the panel of assessors. Having read them, Graham rang me to say that he was extremely embarrassed. While he still thought that Vincent McDonnell's talents deserved recognition, he also praised *The Book of Evidence* by John Banville. Would it be possible to split the £50,000 prize, awarding two prizes instead of one, in accordance with the letter of 9 March 1989.

I contacted Sean Donlon who spontaneously made the offer to create a 'First Fiction Prize' of £20,000 to be awarded to Vincent McDonnell, while the main GPA Literary Award would be conferred on John Banville. Graham heartily approved this generous move that assuaged his scruples.

This simple and straightforward agreement was later distorted and the media accused Graham of reprehensible shenanigans. The media feeding frenzy was such that Vincent Mc Donnell contemplated refusing the award. A curt message was sent to him by Max Reinhardt, publisher of his *Broken Commandment*: 'Graham Greene tells me that that you might refuse the Literary Prize which he was flying to Dublin to present to you. If you do it would be most unfair to him and to your publisher who hoped to sell more copies as a result. Please reconsider your decision as otherwise you will be upsetting many friends'.[3]

Because of the increasingly nasty tone of the controversy, John Banville also felt ill at ease. The solution put forward with great generosity by Guinness Peat Aviation eventually convinced both writers to accept the Award.

---

[3] Judith Adamson, *Max Reinhardt: A Life in Publishing* (London: Palgrave Mac Millan, 2009), 181.

On 28 November 1989, both awards were presented by Desmond O'Malley, Minister for Industry and Commerce, at a dinner in the House of Lords, Bank of Ireland, on College Green in Dublin. Mr O'Malley congratulated the winners and expressed profound thanks to GPA for their support for Irish literature, noting that their award could now be considered the greatest in the world, not only in financial terms, 'but because of the great adjudicator here tonight'. John Banville recited a poem and Graham Greene claimed that 'Irish literature has been the backbone of English literature'.[4] Far from being cold-shouldered, as lazy journalists reported, Graham received a standing ovation from the large audience.

Graham Greene, John Banville, Tony Ryan and Desmond O'Malley, GPA Book Award, 28 November 1989.

Among the guests who heartily applauded him was Lord Gerry Fitt with whom Graham had such a frightening experience in Northern Ireland

4   Kathy Sheridan, 'Banville wins £50.000 GPA Award', *The Irish Times*, 29 November 1989.

in 1977. He had asked GPA to invite Fitt to the literary event in College Green. Fitt had accepted with a wink: 'Sure, I'll go to Dublin and have a jar with Graham'. Fitt, ever the court jester, entertained the literary set with his endless fund of jokes and anecdotes, pretty much unprintable, and a witty poem about King James and King Billy, the two English monarchs who started the Irish troubles.[5]

Graham Greene speaking at the GPA Book Award, Dublin 28 November 1989.

The success of the evening did not quench the media firestorm. At regular intervals, Greene would be excoriated for his 'capricious conduct' as adjudicator. A scathing attack came, more than three years after Graham's death, from Gerry Dukes, administrator of the award. I was astonished by his petulant denunciation, as Dukes had published in *The Irish Times* of 5 April 1991 a warm obituary notice of the Grand Old Man of English letters. In the last paragraph of his eulogy, after having recalled his first visit

5   *The Sunday Tribune*, 3 December 1989.

to Antibes, he wrote with apparent sincerity: 'I met him twice more in Antibes later in the year and then again in Dublin. He was affable, engaging and acerbic – like his books, in fact. He was a pleasure to eat with, to drink with and to listen to. It was a privilege to have known him and now that he has gone a distinguished and distinctive voice in the concord of literature has been stilled'.[6]

In the letter from Gerry Dukes published in the *London Review of Books* of 7 July 1994, the privilege had suddenly been replaced by vituperative acrimony against a sinister character accused of being 'an expert wool merchant', a 'foolish' old man full of 'vanity', complaining endlessly about his health when his only discomfort had been 'the upward pressure on his buttocks from the passenger seats of limousines, a helicopter and an executive jet during his trip to Dublin for the Award'.[7] I found this nasty mockery nauseating. Graham was extremely tired prior to his departure and despite the comfort of his travel arrangements, he returned to Antibes in a state of near exhaustion. Having escorted him on this visit to Co. Tipperary and Dublin, where he received an exceptionally hospitable welcome from Dr Tony Ryan, chairman of GPA, and his team, it was only too obvious that Graham was in considerable pain.

If Dukes was so outraged and horrified by Graham's conduct, why did he not dissociate himself from the entire affair and return GPA's cheque? His vitriolic epistle failed to mention the ovation received by Graham from a large, distinguished and representative Irish audience. Gerry Dukes may have resented this ovation. He may even have remained seated in protest at what he describes rather bluntly as the 'vanity', 'foolishness', 'mischievousness', 'absence of integrity' of the man he had so much pleasure eating and drinking with, and listening to not so long ago. If he did so, I must say that his dissent was so discreet that it went unnoticed.

I wrote to the *London Review of Books* to offer a riposte to these mean and misleading claims, published 22 September 1994. I quoted Jonathan

---

6   Gerry Dukes, 'Travels to Greeneland', *The Irish Times*, 5 April 1991.
7   *The London Review of Books*, 7 July 1994.

Swift: 'When a true genius appears in the world, you may know him by this sign, that the dunces are all in confederacy against him.'[8]

Sean Donlon was upset by this denigration, but the former Ambassador was more courteous in his disapproval than me: 'I am at a loss to explain the discrepancy between my account of Greene and the GPA Book Award and accounts which have appeared elsewhere suggesting an element of Greene mischief, particularly in relation to giving the prize to Mc Donnell.

In my conversations with Greene during his three days in Ireland, he frequently commented favourably on Banville's writings with which he seemed to be familiar. He also expressed great admiration for Seamus Heaney (...) In donating his own fee to Mc Donnell, he was signifying his personal support for a young writer whose first book he had arranged to have published. It was a generous and straightforward gesture – like so many things in Greene's life, there had to be an element of mystery and room for controversy!'[9]

Of this short journey to Ireland with Graham and Yvonne, I retain three lasting memories: the transfer by helicopter from Dublin Airport to Kilboy House in county Tipperary where we received the warmest welcome from Tony Ryan and Lady Miranda Iveagh; Graham's appreciation of his standing ovation in the old Irish Parliament on College Green, following which he said to me, tongue in cheek, 'It is better than being awarded the Nobel prize'; and his pilgrimage to the grave of Jonathan Swift in St Patrick's Cathedral.

Graham would have been only too happy to appropriate Swift's Latin epitaph which translates: 'Here lies the body of Jonathan Swift, Doctor of Divinity and Dean of this Cathedral, where savage indignation can no longer lacerate his heart. Go traveller and imitate, if you can, this dedicated and earnest champion of liberty. He died on the 19th of October 1745, aged 78 years.'

---

8   *The London Review of Books*, 22 September 1994.
9   Sean Donlon, 'Graham Greene and the GPA Book Award' in *Franco-Irish Connections*, 81.

The journey exerted an exacting toll on his health. Indeed, Graham felt exhausted, as Father Leopoldo Duran revealed in his book of reminiscences: 'He returned from Ireland worn out both physically and mentally. When his illness became irreversible, he told me more than once: "Ireland killed me"'.[10]

---

10   Duran, *Graham Greene Friend and Brother*, 277.

Last Encounter

Toward the end of 1989, I was dismayed to discover that Graham's health was indeed deteriorating rapidly. We learned later that he was suffering from aplastic anaemia and needed a series of blood transfusions. He was becoming more and more feeble. He could eat very little. Our encounters were shorter, but no less cordial for that. I met him for the last time in September 1990, shortly before he left for Switzerland to be near his daughter and close to the hospital and doctor who was treating him. On this last occasion, there were no dry martinis, no Jameson whiskeys. But the conversation was as fascinating as ever. I asked him if he knew that his good friend Norman Douglas had lived in Antibes in 1941, renting a room at n°1 Place Macé – now Place de Gaulle. He smiled gently and rose to get a book on the shelves of his library. It was a five hundred pages biography of Norman Douglas by Mark Holloway published in 1976 by Secker and Warburg in London. He handed it to me, saying: 'You will find all the details in this book. Please keep it as a souvenir'. Shortly afterwards we parted on the landing of the fourth floor of the Résidence des Fleurs. I knew that I would never see him again.

Back home, I opened the Norman Douglas biography which Graham had given me as a farewell present. I was overcome to see that it had been presented to him by Catherine Walston, his great love and the inspiration for *The End of the Affair*. It was inscribed in red ink: 'To Graham for Christmas 1976. What fun lunches we had with those three – one especially. Love. Catherine'. Underneath, Graham had scribbled in his minuscule hand: 'Yes, indeed,' followed by the names 'Norman, Kenneth and Islay', making reference to Norman Douglas, Kenneth Macpherson and Islay Lyons. From between the pages fell a photograph of Norman Douglas smoking his pipe in Capri and a card reproducing the *Portrait of the Artist's Brother Diego* by Alberto Giacometti that had a strange resemblance to Graham. Catherine Walston on the reverse had written these few lines on 14 December 1976:

Dearest Graham,

I don't like your water colour in *The Times* but I daresay it's hard to reproduce a watercolour in a newspaper. I really like this picture of YOU and if I had any money and it was not in a USA collection I would have bought it. Don't you like it? But then on the whole I like Giacometti, especially when it looks like you. I hope you have not already bought this book. I read it first as I'm too broke to buy two copies.

Love
Catherine

On 25 October, Graham Greene left Antibes, never to return. After having received a book that I had edited on Dublin from 1904 to 1924, he dropped me a note on 4 March, one month before he died, saying: 'I am stuck here indefinitely forbidden to travel so as to be near the doctor and hospital who are treating me (...) I look forward to reading your own book but it will take me a long time to read as my eyes are bad and I read very little at a time. We miss you and Annick and hope that we shall see you again before too long, but I don't expect to be back in Antibes for some months if then. Lots of love to you both. Graham.'[1] They were his last words to Annick and me, like an affectionate wave, a discreet goodbye.

Three days later, he sent a farewell letter to the Mayor of Antibes, Pierre Merli: 'It is with great sadness that I am writing this letter to tell you that I have been forced to change my residence from France to Switzerland because of my health. For two years now I have been living between one blood transfusion and another, close to the hospital and the doctor who has been treating me since my first attack when I was visiting my daughter here. But there seems to be little hope for change. I am strictly forbidden to travel. Indeed, it is not easy for me to walk more than a few yards on my own. I was very happy in Antibes, the only town in the Côte d'Azur where I could have borne to live, because we had a Mayor who preserved the character of the town, morally and architecturally. I am keeping my flat there in the rather vain hope that one day I may be able to return.'[2]

---

1   Graham Greene to Pierre Joannon, 4 March 1991.
2   Graham Greene to Pierre Merli, 7 March 1991: 'La dernière lettre manuscrite de Graham Greene adressée au maire', *Nice-Matin*, 23 July 1991.

It was a forlorn hope, as Graham knew only too well. He died, aged 86, on 3 April 1991.

However, this was not the end of my association with the man who, for twenty-five years, had been writing in long hand, in front of the sea and the Fort Carré, such masterpieces as *Can We Borrow Your Husband*, *Travels with my Aunt*, *A Sort of Life*, *The Honorary Consul*, his favourite novel, *The Human Factor*, *Doctor Fischer of Geneva*, *Ways of Escape*, *Monsignor Quixote*, *The Captain and the Enemy*, and more.

With the encouragement of the Mayor of Antibes, the support of the family and the help of dedicated friends, I curated a major exhibition on Graham's life and works at the Picasso Museum in the historic Château Grimaldi overlooking the ramparts of Antibes. Launched on 2 October 1992 to coincide with Graham's birthday, this moving tribute, scheduled for one month, proved so successful that it was extended until the end of December. Apart from exhibits borrowed from the British Council and the Editions Robert Laffont, there was a varied selection of private letters, manuscripts, books, paintings, limited editions, poems, decorations such as the Order of Merit bestowed upon him by Queen Elizabeth II, mementoes of his journeys to Russia and South America, photographs, and personal belongings, lent by his family and close friends.

Particularly moving was the manuscript of the yet unpublished *A World of My Own: A Dream Diary*, and a small piece of paper on which Graham had scribbled his five last written words: 'in search of a beginning'. All these memorabilia had never before been seen – and never again will be seen – in public.

On 18 September 1992, a marble plaque bearing the words 'Graham Greene lived here from 1966 to 1990' was unveiled by Mayor Pierre Merli, Yvonne Cloetta and myself, on the façade of the Résidence des Fleurs, 26 Avenue Pasteur. It is now a literary landmark establishing Antibes as the capital of Greeneland, this distinctive and enigmatic body of work on the unsolvable mystery of the human condition beyond any historical or psychological explanation.

Graham was particularly lucid when he scribbled the following words in 1949: 'If anybody ever tries to write a biography of me, how complicated they are going to find it and how misled they are going to be.'

Needless to say, this short témoignage does not aim to be a comprehensive biography. It offers only a collection of reminiscences, impressions, and interpretations. I have tried as honestly as I could to capture, with unabashed empathy, my sense of this volatile, sensitive, complex and consummate novelist during the last twenty years of his life. It brings to my mind the confession full of humility given to us thirteen hundred years ago by Muirchu, the biographer of St Patrick: 'My skill is small, my authorities are uncertain; my memory is treacherous; my intelligence is worn out; my style is poor; yet the feeling of my love is most pious'.[3]

Plaque on the façade of the Résidence des Fleurs, 26 Avenue Pasteur, Antibes.

3   Oliver St John Gogarty, *I Follow St Patrick* (London: Rich & Cowan, 1938), vii.

My memories of Graham in his reflective old age are at odds with the caricature painted by detractors and surprisingly bitter biographers of him as acerbic, calculating, and crabby. The tormented 'man within' had matured in mellowness. At home on the fourth floor of the Résidence des Fleurs, lovingly cared for by his devoted partner Yvonne Cloetta, he found himself, if one put aside the *J'accuse* episode, in a haven of contentment and serenity, though he never lost his capacity for indignation about the sorry state of world affairs. With Annick and me, he was always relaxed, witty, courteous, and attentive.

When I raise my eyes towards the small terrace of his apartment overlooking the harbour of Antibes and the Fort Carré, it is with melancholic nostalgia that I recall our numerous conversations and remember with fond affection the gifted writer friend who, at what would have been his great disbelief, has reached the shores of posthumous immortality as an icon of greatness, for all time.

Interviews and Obituaries: Graham Greene's Other Island

PIERRE JOANNON: Your first visit to Ireland was in 1923, just after the civil war; What were your impressions?

Graham Greene: It seems very distant now. I went with a cousin and we walked from Dublin to Waterford. The impression remain of broken bridges all the way along the route. It was a week after De Valera had issued his order to dump arms. We didn't find any enmity except in one town where people threw a few stones at us on the road and in a pub where the owner pretended that there was no food, although we could notice people eating eggs and bacon. That was all. As a young undergraduate, I had no introduction whatsoever. We knew nobody. We did stop at the house of, I think it was, the poet Katharine Tynan on our way down. She was living quite contentedly in a rather big house but she was boycotted by the local people who claimed that there was a ghost in her drive. They didn't wish to offend her by giving any other reason. But of course, it is very dim in my memory now. I wrote an article in a paper called *The Saturday Westminster* which was a very good weekly paper of the period: I suppose it was one of the first things that I ever got published.

P.J.: Later on, you were a frequent visitor to Achill Island?

G.G.: Yes, at the end of the forties and in the early fifties, I used to go nearly every year to Achill with a friend who had a little fisherman's cottage. There I met Ernie O'Malley, the author of *On Another Man's Wound* who had been Assistant Chief of Staff of the IRA in 1922. He was an enchanting man. I remember, one day in Achill, I asked him at what time high tide was. He hesitated a long time, a look of caution came into his eyes and his attitude became typical of the Old IRA man determined not to give any information to a possible enemy. "Well Graham, that depends", said he laconically in the end.

P.J.: *You went to Northern Ireland in 1977 to see the present troubles for yourself. Again, what were your impressions?*

G.G.: I was horrified. It was to me a situation far worse than the one I had experienced during the London Blitz. How people could go on living under that tension is something I found really extraordinary. I saw people from all sides. I met the Protestant Bishop of Londonderry. I spent a long day with Gerry Fitt whom I admire extremely. I met a senior member of the Alliance Party, an Irish poet, some students and scholars, businessmen, etc…

I remember particularly a Catholic priest from the Falls with whom I talked. He warned me that the little boys in the streets playing marbles would be noting the number of the car in which I was travelling because any newcomer, especially if he was using a government car, would be almost automatically regarded as a CID man. One of the horrifying things which he pointed out was the hardship borne by the young girls of the Falls area. In the normal course before the bad troubles began, a girl would find a boy-friend, Catholic probably, but if she hadn't, she would move outside her ghetto area and find a boy-friend among the Protestants. Now that was utterly impossible, and some of these poor girls had nothing to do in the evenings. One day, a young woman came to him and said 'Father, can't you arrange something for me to do, I can't bear doing nothing every night.' He suggested that she should help him with the small children in the evening. Then he realised what was really troubling her was a sex matter, being imprisoned in the Falls, unable to make contacts, and he had to stop her coming because she was imposing her shattered nerves on the small children. That was an aspect which had never occurred to me.

Another thing which struck me was that the pubs in Belfast all had closed doors and closed windows. There was one particular pub I wanted to go because it had been used as a setting by Carol Reed in his film *Odd Man Out*. Furthermore, it was one of the most attractive pubs of Belfast. I went there with some young men of the University and we knocked on the door. When it opened, we saw that the pub was full but they tried to close the door in our faces because our faces were unfamiliar and they were afraid. We managed to convey that we just wanted to look at the interior because of the film and they grudgingly let us in to take a look. We then had to leave. We were strangers. And any stranger was dangerous.

P.J.: As a stranger, did you have the feeling that you were personally in danger?

G.G.: Well, I felt uneasy because I was an English Catholic with little sympathy for the Provisional IRA Also, as you know, I had been in the Secret Service during the war and people wrongly say that one never leaves the Secret Service. Last but not least, I was lent a government car by the then Labour Government because I had asked for facilities to see the situation for myself. I had a Protestant driver who didn't encourage me to take risks: he too remarked that I would probably be taken for a CID man. He would drive me a little way into the Falls area, then he would stop the car and say he had better not go any further because after this point it would be difficult to turn if there was any trouble. The menace was not one-sided. One of my contacts in government suggested that I should see Andy Tyrie, commander of the UDA, the paramilitary Protestant organization. I mentioned this to my driver as there was only one day left for me to do it and I suggested: "Tomorrow we're going to visit Andy Tyrie". He hesitated and grumbled: "Well I hope he doesn't recognize me". He seemed so anxious that I said: "Well, if this is so we won't visit Andy Tyrie. I am going away, but you are staying".

In a curious way, I found Belfast more threatening that Londonderry. Partly because there was a very obvious military presence in Londonderry. Londonderry was sad, but the local authorities were doing their best with music played through loud speakers in the streets to give at least an air of gaiety. What rather shocked one when one entered Derry was a huge notice on a wall giving you a telephone number to ring up if you had any information to give anonymously. It was the atmosphere depicted by Liam O'Flaherty in *The Informer*. But in Belfast there was not an evident military presence except in the cordon shutting off the centre of the city, and I personally found it more frightening because I had the feeling that what was going to happen was going to be unexpected and probably uncontrolled.

What was my astonishment when, coming down by train to Dublin, I saw young people lying in the grass in St Stephen's Green, courting each other, reading, playing, sleeping, in an atmosphere of peace that one had lost completely during the troubles in the North.

P.J.: Being a Catholic yourself, and furthermore an English Catholic (I do not say a Catholic writer as I hate this label just as much as you do), do you feel a particular responsibility or a particular interest as far as the Irish problem is concerned? Do you see it in the light of the "religious war" so often referred to in the popular press?

G.G.: Well, I certainly feel a personal interest as an Englishman and as a Catholic, and I always have. I had a romantic feeling for the Old IRA as a boy and for Ireland's struggle for independence. But I think the position today is very different: I can't see any real link between the Provos and the Old IRA I can see no links with a man like Michael Collins who was a hero in my youth. I can see no links with the idealism of a man like Erskine Childers.

In Belfast, the easiest way of getting about is to hire a taxi though you don't take a taxi to yourself, you rather 'join' a taxi in which you find yourself with four or five people and possibly a chicken, and pay only your share of the price. Well, I was warned not to take a taxi, because all the taxis were owned by the Provos (I suppose that is why the authorities lent me a car). Most of the big self-service stores were also owned by the Provos. Many small shopkeepers, including Catholics, had ben kneecapped because they had refused to pay protection money. It seemed to me that the new Provo IRA was closer to the Chicago gangsters than to the idealism of men like Erskine Childers and my friend Ernie O'Malley.

Furthermore, it can be said that the Old IRA had a mandate from the people. In the General Election of December 1918, out of 105 candidates returned for Ireland, 73 were Republicans. Actually the Provos have no such mandate. They despise the ballot because the electors do not favour them. And I don't think that the election of Bobby Sands in the Fermanagh-South Tyrone by-election invalidates this argument. The result was exaggerated by the emotional effects of the hunger strike and the deliberately false assumption that to elect him was the only way to save his life. One wonders what would have happened if the SDLP had run a candidate. To offer a choice only between a Catholic Provo and a hard-line Protestant was unfair to the Catholic population. And there may have been also a good deal of terror at work in the figures: in a situation like that, one would have been afraid to abstain from voting, and who can say that there was no intimidation at the polling station?

Now, to answer to the last part of your question 'How far is there a religious element in the situation?', my opinion is that religion is being used as a mean of propaganda or the description of a social condition. The UDA and the Provos are not engaged in a religious war. It is a war of political power and what goes with political power: money.

P.J.: You were enraged by the sheer hypocrisy of the concept of clean torture forged by Mr Reginald Maudling. And you didn't hesitate to launch a fierce attack against him in a letter to the editor of The Times *dated November 26, 1971, which was reproduced in* The New York Times *dated December 2, 1971 (…). Was it the only time when you felt uneasy or even ashamed by the methods used by the British Army or the Royal Ulster Constabulary? Do you think that, on this front, things have improved in 1981?*

G.G.: Right now, I don't know enough to say whether or how much it has improved as far as the police is concerned. I feel the Army has been in an unhappy situation and I don't feel much blame can be attached to the Army. They were put in to protect the Catholic population. The situation wasn't as clear at the time when I wrote that letter as it is today. The Chicago element was not nearly so evident. The civil authorities were behaving very badly. For instance, I found that internment without trial was one of the things which antagonized most the Catholics who were not Provos in Belfast when I was there. A senior member of the Alliance Party, who was in fact a Protestant, told me that when he was a school boy he used to notice that the sixteen years old boy who sat next to him at school would disappear every now and then. The reason was that he had a grand-father who had been in the IRA in the good old days, if I can call them that, and whenever a member of the Royal Family or a senior member of the Government visited Northern Ireland, he would be interned with his father who had never been in the IRA, just because the record showed that his grand-father had been, and he would lose a week's lessons. I gathered that the Army had been very much against that policy of internment without trial at the time of Maudling and it seemed to me an absurd law which could have been easily repealed from whatever emergency legislation had been passed in the twenties. And that would have made a great difference, I think, to the feelings of the Catholics who were anti-Provo. But I must confess that I don't know what the situation is today, I am completely out of date.

P.J.: The last part of your letter to the Editor of The Times *is worth quoting: "And after all the British torture and the Catholic outrages, what comes next? We all know the end of the story, however long the politics keep up their parrot cry of 'no talk until violence ends'. When I was young it was the same cliché they repeated. Collins was 'a gunman and a thug'. 'We will not talk to murderers'. No one doubts that it was in our power then to hold Ireland by force. The Black and Tans matched the Republicans in terror. It was the English people who in the end forced the politicians to sit down at a table with 'the gunman and the thug'. Now too, when the deaths and the tortures have gone on long enough to blacken us in the eyes of the world and to sicken even a Conservative of the right, there will inevitably be a temporary truce and a round-table conference. Mr Maudling or his successor will sit down over the coffee and the sandwiches with representatives of Eire and Stormont, of the IRA and the Provisional IRA, to discuss with no pre-ordained conditions changes in the constitution and in the borders of Ulster. Why not now rather than later?" Is this statement of yours still valid after ten years or would you say that you have changed your mind?*

G.G.: I feel the situation was very different when I was writing. I don't think that I would say now that it would end inevitably around the Conference table. I think like Conor Cruise O'Brien that a redrawing of the Border should be considered but I don't think the Republic particularly want that, do they? Also I do not think that Britain should leave Northern Ireland precipitately. I do think that the troops are necessary there for the time being. My opinion has rather altered since Maudling's time, I must say, with the course of events and the increase of atrocities and terrorism. At the time when I wrote that letter, terrorism was not so extreme and I think there was a certain idealism left which I no longer believe in on either side. The Provos are not even supported by their own countrymen in Eire with whom they say they share the same spiritual Republican faith.

P.J.: *In* Doctor Fischer of Geneva, *your hero is tempted to commit suicide. Among the various means to kill himself, he contemplates starvation and quotes the example of Terence Mc Swiney, the Lord Mayor of Cork, adding: "after all, starvation might perhaps be the proper answer, a clean and discreet and private way out". How about the hunger strike as a much publicized and public way out? As a Catholic and as a man with a vast experience of – and should I say sympathy for – political dissent all over the world, what is your opinion on the hunger strike for political motives, and especially on the systematic campaign of hunger strike which caused the death of Bobby Sands and his companions in 1981?*

G.G.: As a Catholic, I don't agree with one of the condemnations of the Catholic Church regarding these hunger strikes. I don't think that a hunger strike is what used to be called a mortal sin. Theologically, suicide was regarded as a mortal sin because it was an expression of despair, but to kill yourself by hunger striking is not an expression of despair and I think theologically the Cardinal is perfectly correct in not condemning it. What I think is very condemnable is to allow hooded men in uniforms to fire with guns at a funeral. I would like to see it made a condition of a hunger striker being buried properly in a cemetery that no armed men should be on the scene. But I am not against hunger striking as such. I don't object to it as a method of protest, I only object to the cause in this case. There is another point. What is the psychological condition of the hunger striker as he approaches death? Who are by his bedside? If he wishes to change his mind towards the end, what are the pressures on him to continue? Is he a master of himself or is he a puppet?
Terence Mc Swiney was fighting a good fight, Bobby Sands wasn't. For a young English boy of that period the sacrifice of the Lord Mayor of Cork was part of a very romantic revolution against imperialist England.

P.J.: You rightly recall that a large sector of British public opinion was very hostile to the government during the Black and Tans war, which is apparently not the case with the present troubles in Northern Ireland.

G.G.: Yes, the opposition was very strong in the twenties. Indeed, it was the protests of the English conscience which forced the government to withdraw the Black and Tans. As far as I am concerned, I suppose I always had a sympathy with attacks on British colonialism. There is a very fine open poem by Wilfrid Scawen Blunt who was not an Irishman though he espoused the Irish cause in the 1880s and went to prison in Ireland for his opposition, called "The Wind and the Whirlwind" which I always found very attractive, especially these lines about the defeat of the Egyptian leader by the British troops:

> I care not if you fled. What men call courage
> Is the least noble thing of which they boast.

And then it goes on:
> Oh I would rather fly with the first craven
> Who flung his arms away in your good cause
> Than head the hottest charge by England vaunted
> In all the record of her unjust wars.

P.J.: What is the historical or political figure that you admire most in the Ireland of today or in the last sixty years or so? As for the character whom you hate most, I suspect that it is the Reverend Paisley which you describe to Marie-Françoise Allain in a fine book of interviews entitled L'Autre et son Double *(Belfond, 1981) as the "abominable Paisley". Abominable in what sense: like Pinkie in* Brighton Rock *who, according to the priest, might be saved at the last minute, or rather like Papa Doc or Hitler, hopeless cases for which you commend the most radical treatment: murder?*

G.G.: In a way, Hitler seems to me such an obvious madman that perhaps he wins mercy in the end. Paisley is not mad. I could play you one of his sermons which I taped while I was in Belfast. He talks about himself as the Reverend Dr. Paisley, head of a branch of the Presbyterian Church which he has invented himself. I think he is an abominable man.

A protestant bishop told me a story about him. He was a young curate in Belfast at the time. News came to his ears that there was likely to be an attack on a Catholic area by Orangemen, and with a large number of protestant clergy he formed a human barrier at the entrance of the Falls with linked arms. Then suddenly a lot of drunken Orangemen with sticks appeared with the intention of marching in. They were faced by their own Protestant clergy and that made them hesitate. Finally they began to break up into little groups and the danger passed. After the danger was over, a tall figure in a mackintosh arrived at the back and said: "Come, follow me fellows, this is not the way to deal with the Catholics" and marched them away. Of course, it was Ian Paisley. This is a story I like. Some are less amusing. For instance, it is difficult to forget that in June 1966, long before the actual troubles began, four young Catholic barmen were riddled with bullets at the Watson's Bar in Malvern Street in the Protestant Shankill area. These sectarian murders were perpetrated by members of the Ulster Volunteer Force, a body publicly associated with Paisley. One of the murderers said at his trial: "I am sorry I ever heard tell of that man Paisley or decided to follow him".

P.J.: That is true, but on the other hand, you are probably aware of the fact that Mr Paisley is at present one of the most popular, if not the most popular, political figures among Northern Irish Protestants.

G.G.: Yes, and I am sure his church is full all the time. It has thick carpets on the floor. It is one of the most comfortable churches that I have ever seen. Also Paisley runs his own printing press, prints his own sermons. Above all, he is the one man who is safest, I would think, in Northern Ireland. Nobody will ever kill him, not the Provos certainly, because he is their greatest ally. He can walk from one end of Ireland to the other unarmed and without an escort, nobody will hurt him, unfortunately.

Now, you asked me what were the historical figures I admired most in the history of modern Ireland. Well, I have got a sentimental feeling for Parnell, much more than for Redmond for example. For Michael Collins again I had a rather romantic admiration which was due also to the fact that he was a very good guerrilla fighter. I also admired Erskine Childers for his novel *The Riddle of the Sands*, and for his integrity, and perhaps the fact that he was shot by his former companions added to his glamour. De Valera has never somehow caught my imagination.

P.J.: You have set many novels in troubled lands: Mexico in The Power and the Glory; *Haiti in* The Comedians; *Vietnam in* The Quiet American; *Cuba in* Our Man in Havana, *etc. But Ireland never inspired you. Why?*

G.G.: I don't know. Maybe because I have never spent enough time in Ireland. And maybe because Ireland was on my doorstep. It's like somebody who lives in a city, a visitor comes, and he begins to see his city for the first time. One doesn't know the things on one's doorstep. Which is one of the reasons why I went to Belfast. It was absurd: I had been in Malaya during the Emergency, in Kenya during the Mau Mau rebellion, in Vietnam during the French war, and I had not even taken a look at what was going on next door. But it wouldn't be enough to take a look, I would have to stay a long time to write a book.

P.J.: Ireland is too close. Maybe this is why the "Irish question" was and still is so largely ignored or misunderstood by the English people. Would you agree?

G.G.: As far as politics are concerned, that is perhaps true. But not as far as literature is concerned. Irish writers probably had a better audience in England than in Southern Ireland, partly due to the censorship there. Incidentally, four of my books were banned in Ireland: *The Heart of the Matter, The End of the Affair, England Made Me* and *The Quiet American.* But in each case, the appeal was successful. Anyhow, I suspect that James Joyce, Elizabeth Bowen, Yeats, Shaw, Flann O'Brien even, probably had their biggest audience in England. So the English do read about Ireland. They are not so ignorant.

P.J.: Fair enough, but in your works, and especially in your Essays *you seldom mention Irish authors or Irish literature as a possible source of influence or even interest. Is it by inadvertence or are you totally cut off from the Irish stream of culture?*

G.G.: It is purely accidental. My *Essays* are based on reviews and the books I reviewed were the choice of the editor. I never reviewed poetry and therefore I have never written about Yeats whom I consider with Hardy as the two greatest poets of my lifetime. Joyce I always admired especially for his short stories. Elizabeth Bowen also, and Flann O'Brien: I claim to have been with Joyce one of the two writers who wrote about his first book *At Swim two birds* at some length. Twenty one years later, I was much honoured to open a book of his, because I always bought his books, and find a dedication in it. It was *The Hard Life* and the dedication runs thus: "I honourably present to Graham Greene whose own form of gloom I admire, this misterpiece". No, the Irish culture has always meant a great deal to me. There are innumerable poets I admire even going back to James Clarence Mangan. And one of my favourite novelists now is Brian Moore who has settled in America but who comes from Northern Ireland. Perhaps his best work was done when he was writing about Northern Ireland. Another Irish writer has been a life-long friend of mine, Sean O'Faolain, whom I saw when I went to Dublin after Belfast. We went on a pilgrimage to the Martello tower of Joyce together. As far as painting is concerned, I am a great admirer of Jack B. Yeats and the proud possessor of two of his later works. I am also very fond of another less known Irish painter, Roderic O'Conor who was a friend of Gauguin. He was with him in Brittany and Gauguin invited him to go with him to the South Seas. But he didn't go and continued to work in Paris where he had a studio. I have got one of his pictures which I like very much, a woman combing her hair in front of a mirror, which is very near to Bonnard.

P.J.: Do you know the story told by Ann Crookshank and the Knight of Glin in their marvellous book on The Painters of Ireland. *After O'Conor refused to accompany Gauguin on his second visit to Tahiti, he replied to his friend Alden Brooks, when asked why he did not go, "No, but do you see me going to the South Seas with that character!"*

G.G.: Well anyway, he went to Gauguin's rescue when he was attacked by drunken sailors in Concarneau where, incidentally, I had the best coquilles Saint Jacques I ever tasted.

P.J.: One of your favourite authors is G.K. Chesterton. As far as the "Irish Question" is concerned, Chesterton was a liberal. He protested loudly against the policy of reprisals carried out by the Black and Tans and wrote two pamphlets for the Peace with Ireland Council. In his Autobiography *he writes: "I have always felt it the first duty of a real English patriot to sympathise with the passionate patriotism of Ireland". He also wrote, speaking as an Englishman: "The two nations that are nearest are those we never understand: Ireland and France". Do you agree? And would you say that as an Englishman and as a Catholic yourself, you are following G.K.'s tracks as far as Ireland is concerned?*

G.G.: I admire Chesterton very much. He had a very romantic vision of Ireland and Irishmen. He was inclined to see them all redheaded and rather crazy. I don't think I share this idea of an Irishman, although I am sure that Chesterton would have appreciated Ernie O'Malley's caution over the tide.

I don't know whether we will ever understand the Irish. I seem to understand the Irish when I am reading Irish writers. I never have the feeling that I am not understanding the Irish when I read Irish books, anymore than I have the feeling that I am not understanding the French when I read French books. I don't understand this business of a mysterious nationality. I think that was part of Chesterton's romanticism.

As for France, I visited it all by myself for the first time when I was 19 years old and fell in love with the country. I used to come and have a 'wine walk' in Burgundy with a brother once a year before the war. So I feel it is perfectly natural now to be ending my days in France.

Pierre Joannon, 'Graham Greene's Other Island', *Etudes Irlandaises* (6 December 1981), 157–69.

The Sage of Antibes

I knew that I would never see him again. He had left before Christmas for Switzerland in order to be near his daughter and close to the doctor and the hospital who were treating him. He didn't have any illusion though. He knew perfectly well that there was not much hope left. This indomitable man who had always been on the move – one day in Moscow, the next in London or Panama – who was still reading the papers with a juvenile voracity, receiving and annotating books, answering phone calls from all over the world and specially from his beloved South America, had suddenly ceased making plans for the future. He had the sad sort of smile and the frail, estranged look, of a man about to leave never to return.

He first came to Antibes in 1946 to sail with Alexander Korda, the film producer, who kept a boat in the harbour. He fell in love with the little Mediterranean city. So much so that when, having contracted pneumonia in Russia, he was advised to spend the winters in milder climate, he decided to rent an apartment near the Ramparts for two months at a time. Getting more and more tired of coming and going back, he decided to reside permanently in Antibes. Typical of him, he made a point of coming by train and not by air to mark the decision. And, on 1 January 1966, he settled in a little two room apartment on the fourth floor of the Résidence des Fleurs which overlooks the harbour.

I was living, at the time, in the same block of flats. One day, that was in 1971, I found the courage to talk to him. He had published in the London *Times* a fierce letter attacking Reginald Maudling on the question of 'clean torture' in Northern Ireland. We had a long, friendly chat on the stairs, followed throughout the years by numerous encounters in his flat, at my home, or at Félix, the restaurant on the harbour where he was lunching practically every day when in Antibes.

Although four of his books had been banned by the Irish Censor, he was extremely fond of Ireland. With a cousin, he had walked from Dublin to Waterford in 1923 shortly after the end of the Civil War. At the beginning of the Fifties, he got into the habit of holidaying every year on Achill Island where he became a close friend of Ernie O'Malley.

In 1977, he visited Belfast to make up his mind about the situation in the North. He was horrified. 'Since I was a teenager, he said to me, I had a romantic leaning towards the Old IRA of the 1920s, and the Irish fight for freedom. Today the situation is very different. I don't see any similarity between the Provisional IRA and the Old IRA There are no bonds between the terrorists of today and the idealists like Erskine Childers or Michael Collins who were heroes in my youth.'

He considered Yeats as the greatest poet of his time. He admired Joyce, particularly for his short stories, and held George Birmingham as one of the greatest humorists in the English language. He had all his books in his library and he insisted that I should read *The Search Party* which, he assured me, was a 'mini-masterpiece'.

He was proud of being one of the very few writers who trumpeted the arrival of Flann O'Brien's first novel *At Swim Two Birds*. He was also very appreciative of Sean O'Faolain, with whom he had made an expedition to Joyce's Martello Tower in the 1970s.

He never refused to attend my Irish parties and I have no doubt that he particularly enjoyed the Irish wit and turn of mind. So much so that I didn't have any difficulty in convincing him to come over to Dublin, in November 1989, to present the GPA Book Award to John Banville and a special first fiction award to Vincent Mc Donnell. The standing ovation that he got at the reception at the House of Lords of the Bank of Ireland moved him to tears. 'It was far better than the Nobel Prize', he said to me afterwards. That was one of his last public appearances, if not the last.

But he struggled until the very end and never lost interest in what was going on around him. Having been told that I had written a book on Dublin during the years 1904–1924, he dropped me a note about three weeks ago: 'I look forward to your own book but it will take me a long time to read it as my eyes are bad and I read very little at a time.' They were to be his last words to me, like a friendly wave of the hand, sending a discreet goodbye.

Today the sun is shining in vain over the Old Ramparts of Antibes. Despite the crowd, there is emptiness in the air. There will be no more drinking parties and book chats at the Résidence des Fleurs.

Pierre Joannon, 'The sage of Antibes', *The Irish Times*, Thursday 4 April 1991.

Our Man in Antibes

Graham Greene isn't dead: he has just slipped off to join some of the elusive characters from his disturbing novels while we weren't paying attention. On a small piece of paper, he left behind a few enigmatic words, which were to be his last: 'In search of a beginning'. Let's hope that the 'Catholic agnostic' he claimed to be has, at last, found the heart of the matter behind the thin veil which separates life from death.

Graham Greene first came to Antibes after the war. In 1966, he settled into a small apartment on the fourth floor of the Résidence des Fleurs, a block of flats overlooking the harbour (…) He was not in exile. He truly loved this Mediterranean spot. After leaving for Switzerland to be near his daughter and close to the hospital and doctor who was treating him, he sent a moving letter to the Mayor of Antibes, Pierre Merli:

'It is with great sadness that I am writing this letter to tell you that I have been forced to change my residence from France to Switzerland because of my health. For two years now I have been living between one blood transfusion and another, close to the hospital and the doctor who has been treating me since my first attack when I was visiting my daughter here. But there seems little hope for change. I am strictly forbidden to travel. Indeed, it is not easy for me to walk more than a few yards on my own. I was very happy in Antibes, the only town on the Côte d'Azur where I could have borne to live, because we had a Mayor who preserved the character of the town, morally and architecturally. I am keeping my flat there in the rather vain hope that one day I may be able to return'.

For almost twenty-five years, facing the sea and the Fort Carré, Greene wrote in long-hand no less than 300 words a day, producing such masterpieces as *Can We Borrow your Husband?* which takes place in Antibes, *Travels with my Aunt*, *A Sort of Life*, *The Honorary Consul* which he considered as his best novel, *The Human Factor*, *Doctor Fischer of Geneva*, *Ways of Escape*, *Monsignor Quixote*, *The Captain and the Enemy*, etc.

From his spartan two-roomed flat overlooking the Port Vauban, Graham Greene was busy writing hundreds of concerned letters to the editors of the world press, annotating books that piled up on his desk, advising young writers and recommending them to his old friend and publisher Max Reinhardt, answering phone calls from places as far apart as Moscow and Panama, and discussing politics and literature with a juvenile passion that I will never forget. I recall with deep emotion the long discussions I had with him over a vodka or martini on Henry James, Conrad, Ford Madox Ford, George Birmingham or Flann O'Brien, who were among his favourite prose writers, and on Yeats, Lawrence Durrell, Kipling and G. K. Chesterton whom he admired greatly as poets.

Antibes was in fact so much part of Graham Greene, and he so much part of the local scene, that the idea of honouring his memory was soon taken up by Mayor Pierre Merli and a handful of friends who succeeded in putting together a major exhibition on his life and works at the Picasso Museum in the Château Grimaldi. Launched on October 2nd to coincide with his birthday – Greene would have been 88 –, this moving tribute has been so successful that it has been extended throughout the month of December.

Apart from exhibits borrowed from the British Council and the Editions Robert Laffont, most of the private letters, manuscripts, books, paintings, decorations such as the Order of Merit bestowed upon him by Queen Elizabeth II, mementoes of his journeys to Russia and South America, rare photographs and personal belongings, were lent by members of the family and very close friends of Graham Greene: they have never been seen in public and will most certainly not be seen again

Last but not least, during the month of December, a plaque will be unveiled on the Résidence des Fleurs as a literary landmark for the countless admirers of the restless Englishman, thanks to whom Antibes has become now and forever the capital of Greeneland.

Pierre Joannon, 'Our Man in Antibes', *New Riviera Côte d'Azur* (Autumn–Winter 1992), 22–23.

Bibliography

Adamson, Judith, *Max Reinhardt: A Life in Publishing* (London: Palgrave Macmillan, 2009).
Barré, Jean-Luc, *François Mauriac: Biographie intime 1885–40* (Paris: Fayard, 2009).
Cash, William, *The Third Woman: The Secret Passion That Inspired The End of the Affair* (London: Little Brown & Company, 2000).
Cassis, A. F., ed., *Graham Greene Man of Paradox: A Collection of Interviews and Impressions by Friends and Contemporaries* (Chicago: Loyola University Press, 1994).
Cloetta, Yvonne, As told to Marie-Françoise Allain, In *Search of a Beginning: My Life with Graham Greene* (London: Bloomsbury, 2004).
Connolly, Cyril, *The Condemned Playground: Essays 1927–44* (London: The Hogarth Press, 1985).
Conroy, Jane, ed., *Franco-Irish Connections: Essays, Memoirs and Poems in Honour of Pierre Joannon* (Dublin: Four Courts Press, 2009).
Craig, Patricia, *Brian Moore: A Biography* (London: Bloomsbury, 2004).
Donaghy, Henry J., ed., *Conversations with Graham Greene* (Jackson and London: University Press of Mississippi, 1992).
Duran, Leopoldo, *Graham Greene Friend and Brother* (London: Harper Collins, 1994).
Green, Julien, *Œuvres Complètes*, Volume IV (Paris: Gallimard, Bibliothèque de la Pléiade, 1975).
Greene, Graham, *The Pleasure Dome: The Collected Film Criticism 1935–40*, edited by John Russell Taylor (London: Secker and Warburg, 1972).
Greene, Graham, *Collected Stories Including May We Borrow Your Husband? A Sense of Reality and Twenty-One Stories* with an introduction by the author (London: The Bodley Head & William Heinemann, 1974).
Greene, Graham, *Ways of Escape* (Toronto: Lester and Orpen Dennys, 1980).
Greene, Graham, *L'Autre et son Double*, entretiens avec Marie-Françoise Allain (Paris: Pierre Belfond, 1981).
Greene, Graham, *J'Accuse: The Dark Side of Nice* (London: The Bodley Head, 1982).
Greene, Graham, *Yours etc. Letters to the Press 1945–89*, selected and introduced by Christopher Hawtree (London: Reinhardt Books, 1989).
Greene, Graham, *Reflections*, selected and introduced by Judith Adamson (London: Reinhardt Books, 1990).

Greene, Graham, *La Chaise Vide et Autres Récits Inédits*, Édition établie et présentée par François Gallix et Isabelle D. Philippe (Paris: Robert Laffont, Collection Bouquins, 2011).

Greene, Richard, ed., *Graham Greene: A Life in Letters* (London: Little Brown, 2007).

Greene, Richard, *Russian Roulette: The Life and Times of Graham Greene* (London: Little Brown, 2020).

Joannon, Pierre, *Michel Mohrt, réfractaire stendhalien* (Paris: Éditions La Thébaïde, 2021).

Krause, David, ed., *The Letters of Sean O'Casey 1955–58*, Volume III (Washington, DC: Catholic University of America Press, 1989).

Leroy, Jean, *Fils de la Rizière*, Préface de Graham Greene (Paris: Robert Laffont, 1977).

Lewis, Jeremy, *Shades of Greene: One Generation of an English Family* (London: Vintage Books, 2010).

Long, Maebh, ed., *The Collected Letters of Flann O'Brien* (Dalkey: Dalkey Archives Press, 2018).

MacArthur, John R., ed., *Graham Greene: The Last Interview and Other Conversations* (Brooklyn and London: Melville House, 2019).

Matthews, Ronald, *Mon Ami Graham Greene* (Paris: Desclée de Brouwer, 1957).

Mc Gahern, John, *Love of the World: Essays* (London: Faber and Faber, 2009).

O'Brien, Conor Cruise, *Maria Cross: Imaginative Patterns in a Group of Catholic Writers* (London: Burns & Oates, 1963).

O'Brien, Conor Cruise, *Memoir: My Life and Themes* (Dublin: Poolbeg Press, 1998).

O'Connor, Ulick, ed., *The Campbell Companion: The Best of Patrick Campbell* (London: Pavilion Books, 1987).

O'Faolain, Julia, *Trespassers: A Memoir* (London: Faber and Faber, 2013).

O'Faolain, Sean, *The Vanishing Hero: Studies in Novelists of the Twenties* (London: Eyre and Spottiswoode, 1956).

O'Faolain, Sean, *Vive Moi! An Autobiography* (London: Sinclair Stevenson, 1993).

Philby, Rufina, *The Private Life of Kim Philby: The Moscow Years* (London: Little Browne & Company, 1999).

Sherry, Norman, *The Life of Graham Greene, Volume I, 1904–39* (London: Jonathan Cape, 1989).

Sherry, Norman, *The Life of Graham Greene, Volume II, 1939–55* (London: Jonathan Cape, 1994).

Sherry, Norman, *The Life of Graham Greene, Volume III, 1955–91* (London: Viking Penguin, 2004).

Smith, Sheamus, *Off Screen: A Memoir* (Dublin: Gill and Macmillan, 2007).

Thomson, Ian, ed., *Articles of Faith: The Collected Tablet Journalism of Graham Greene* (Oxford: Signal Books, 2006).

STUDIES IN FRANCO-IRISH RELATIONS

Series Editor:
Dr Eamon Maher, Technological University Dublin

The aim of this series is to foreground areas of interdisciplinary and multidisciplinary connection between France and Ireland, as well as stressing the European dimension of the Franco–Irish nexus. The series also provides a forum for French-language scholarship within the field of Irish studies.

We welcome proposals from a variety of disciplinary backgrounds, including historical, cultural, literary, sociological, political and linguistic perspectives. The series publishes books in both English and French and all submissions will be peer-reviewed.

Proposals should be sent to
eamon.maher@tudublin.ie or A.Mason@peterlang.com.

L'objectif de cette collection est de valoriser les recherches multi-disciplinaires ou inter-disciplinaires relatives à la France et à l'Irlande, et de souligner la dimension européenne des relations franco-irlandaises. La collection offre également un espace d'échanges pour la recherche francophone en études irlandaises.

Nous accueillons des projets de publication relevant de différents champs disciplinaires et s'inscrivant dans une perspective historique, culturelle, littéraire, sociologique, politique ou linguistique. Les ouvrages de la collection sont publiés en anglais et en français; tous les projets sont soumis à une évaluation par les pairs.

Les propositions peuvent être envoyées à
eamon.maher@tudublin.ie ou à A.Mason@peterlang.com.

Vol. 1   Eamon Maher, Eugene O'Brien and Grace Neville (eds)
          Reinventing Ireland through a French Prism
          ISBN 978-3-631-56639-8. 2007

Vol. 2   Eamon Maher, Grace Neville and Eugene O'Brien (eds)
          Modernity and Postmodernity in a Franco- Irish
          Context
          ISBN 978-3-631-58158-2. 2008

Vol. 3   Yann Bévant, Eamon Maher, Grace Neville and Eugene
          O'Brien (eds)
          Issues of Globalisation and Secularisation in France and
          Ireland
          ISBN 978-3-631-59052-2. 2009

Vol. 4   Déborah Vandewoude
          L'Eglise catholique face aux défis contemporains en
          République d'Irlande. Rédefinition d'une institution
          désacralisée
          ISBN 978-3-631-61897-4. 2012

Vol. 5   Karine Deslandes
          Regards français sur le conflit nord-irlandais
          ISBN 978-3-631-64593-2. 2013

Vol. 6   Chris Reynolds
          Sous les pavés … The Troubles: Northern Ireland,
          France and the European Collective Memory of 1968
          ISBN 978-3-631-62643-6. 2014

Vol. 7   Edwige Nault
          L'avortement en Irlande: 1983–2013. Dimensions
          religieuses, socioculturelles, politiques et européennes
          ISBN 978-3-631-65654-9. 2015

Vol. 8   Janick Julienne
         Un Irlandais à Paris. John Patrick Leonard, au cœur des
         relations franco-irlandaises (1814–1889)
         ISBN 978-1-906165-67-3. 2016

Vol. 9   Frank Healy and Brigitte Bastiat (eds)
         Voyages between France and Ireland. Culture, Tourism
         and Sport
         ISBN 978-3-0343-2264-5. 2017

Vol. 10   Agnès Maillot, Jennifer Bruen and Jean-Philippe Imbert
         (eds)
         Non-Violent Resistance. Irreverence in Irish Culture
         ISBN 978-1-78707-707-2. 2018

Vol. 11   Agnès Maillot and Jennifer Bruen (eds)
         Non-Violent Resistance. Counter-Discourse in Irish
         Culture
         ISBN 978-1-78707-711-9. 2018

Vol. 12   Cécile Maudet
         L'autrefois et l'ailleurs: Poétique de la rupture dans
         l'oeuvre littéraire de Colum McCann
         ISBN 978-1-78874-491-1. 2018

Vol. 13   Fabrice Mourlon
         L'urgence de dire: L'Irlande du Nord après le conflit
         ISBN 978-1-78874-611-3. 2018

Vol. 14   Eamon Maher and Eugene O'Brien (eds) *Patrimoine/
         Cultural Heritage in France and Ireland*
         ISBN 978-1-78874-660-1. 2019

Vol. 15   Catherine Maignant, Sylvain Tondeur and Déborah
           Vandewoude (eds)
           Margins and Marginalities in Ireland and France:
           A Socio-cultural Perspective
           ISBN 978-1-78997-747-9. 2020

Vol. 16   Pierre Ranger and Anne Magny (eds)
           Une révolutionnaire irlandaise en France: Maud Gonne
           et l'internationale nationaliste, 1887–1914
           ISBN 978-1-78874-171-2. 2020

Vol. 17   Bertrand Cardin
           Neil Jordan écrivain-scénariste: L'imaginaire de la
           transgression
           ISBN 978-1-80079-520-4. 2021

Vol. 18   Pierre Costecalde
           Les chaînes de télévisions celtiques face à
           la globalisation: Résistance, convergence et
           déterritorialisations
           ISBN 978-1-80079-493-1. 2022

Vol. 19   Sarah Nolan Balen and Eamon Maher (eds)
           Sounding the Margins: Literary Examples from France
           and Ireland
           ISBN 978-1-78997-748-6. 2022

Vol. 20   Máirtín Mac Con Iomaire and Eamon Maher (eds)
           New Beginnings: Perspectives from France and Ireland
           ISBN 978-1-80079-793-2. 2023

Vol. 21   *Forthcoming*.

Vol. 22   Jeanne-Marie Carton-Charon
           Réception d'Edna O'Brien, Jennifer Johnston, et Nuala
           O'Faolain: Clubs de lecture et forums en ligne / France,
           Irlande, Royaume-Uni et États-Unis
           ISBN 978-1-80374-045-4. 2023

Vol. 23   Pierre Joannon
           Graham Greene, Ireland and the Honorary Consul:
           A View from the South of France
           ISBN 978-1-80374-423-0. 2024

www.ingramcontent.com/pod-product-compliance
Ingram Content Group UK Ltd.
Pitfield, Milton Keynes, MK11 3LW, UK
UKHW021310180426
11947UKWH00015B/1139